TRATAKA

A Concentrated Gazing Technique for Mystical Powers

Prof. (Dr.) Jai Paul Dudeja

Notion Press Media Pvt Ltd

No. 50, Chettiyar Agaram Main Road,
Vanagaram, Chennai, Tamil Nadu – 600 095

First Published by Notion Press 2022
Copyright © Prof. (Dr.) Jai Paul Dudeja 2022
All Rights Reserved.

ISBN 979-8-88606-656-2

This book has been published with all efforts taken to make the material error-free after the consent of the author. However, the author and the publisher do not assume and hereby disclaim any liability to any party for any loss, damage, or disruption caused by errors or omissions, whether such errors or omissions result from negligence, accident, or any other cause.

While every effort has been made to avoid any mistake or omission, this publication is being sold on the condition and understanding that neither the author nor the publishers or printers would be liable in any manner to any person by reason of any mistake or omission in this publication or for any action taken or omitted to be taken or advice rendered or accepted on the basis of this work. For any defect in printing or binding the publishers will be liable only to replace the defective copy by another copy of this work then available.

Contents

Preface *11*
Acknowledgements *13*

Chapter 1: Introduction to Trataka **15**
1.1 Trāṭaka (Concentrated Gazing) Meditation 15
1.2 Trâtaka in Hatha Yoga Pradipika 24
1.3 Trâtaka in Gheranda Samhita 27
1.4 Modes of Trataka Techniques 28
1.5 History of Trataka 32
1.6 Trataka Practices from Different Traditions 41
1.7 Benefits of Trataka 44
1.8 Precautions in doing Trataka 46
1.9 Vision of Purushas and Dreams 47
1.10 Trataka vs. Meditation: What's the Difference? 48

Chapter 2: Trataka on Sun (Sun-Gazing) 51

2.1 Trataka on Sun 51

2.2 About Hira Ratan Manek (HRM), the Famous Sun-Gazer 58

2.3 Step-wise Sun-Gazing Practice for Nine Months 60

2.4 More Benefits of Sun Gazing 67

Chapter 3: Trataka on Moon or Stars (Moon- or Stars-Gazing) 73

3.1 Gazing at the Moon 73

3.2 The Story of the Moon Gazing Hare 74

3.3 Moon-Gazing Meditation 74

3.4 Moon-Gazing or Trataka Technique 75

3.5 Moon-Gazing Benefits 80

3.6 Myth vs. Fact 82

3.7 Potential Risks of Moon-Gazing 83

3.8 Stars-Gazing 83

Chapter 4: Trataka on Candle Flame (Candle-Gazing) 87

4.1 Candle-Gazing 87

4.2 How to Practice Trataka on Candle Flame? 88

4.3 Practice Notes on Candle-Gazing 90

4.4	Benefits of Candle-Gazing	91
4.5	Contraindications: Is Trataka Dangerous?	95
4.6	Parting Thoughts on Candle-Gazing	95

Chapter 5: Agni Trataka (Fire–Gazing) 97

5.1	In Awe of Agni (Fire)	97
5.2	Agni Suktam in Rig Veda	98
5.3	What is Agni Trataka (Fire-Gazing)? Benefits and Precautions	101

Chapter 6: Trataka (Gazing) on Flower or Leaf or Tree 105

6.1	Trataka on a Flower	105
6.2	How To Practice Flower-Gazing Meditation?	107
6.3	Dwelling in the Lotus Heart: A Meditation Practice	110
6.4	Trataka on Leaf	113
6.5	Trataka on Tree	113

Chapter 7: Trataka on Sea or River or Lake (Jala–Trataka) 117

| 7.1 | Trataka on Sea or River (Jala-Trataka) | 117 |
| 7.3 | Trataka Meditation on Lake | 118 |

Chapter 8: Bhrumadhya Drishti (Trataka on the Middle of Eyebrows) 121

- 8.1 What is Shambhavi Mudra & Shambhavi Mahamudra Kriya (Bhrumadhya Drishti)? 121
- 8.2 Shambhavi Mudra (Eyebrow-Centre Gazing) 124
- 8.3 How to do Eyebrow-Centre Gazing? 125
- 8.4 Eyebrow-Centre-Gazing Benefits 130
- 8.5 Precautions in doing Shambhavi Mudra 136

Chapter 9: Nasikagra Drishti (Agochari Mudra): Trataka on Nose Tip 137

- 9.1 Trataka on Nose Tip (Nasikagra Drishti) 137
- 9.2 Gazing at the Nose Tip (Nasikagra Drishti or Agochari Mudra) 138
- 9.3 How to do Nasikagra Drishti (Nose Tip Gazing)? 140
- 9.4 Contra-Indications and Further Instructions of Nose-Tip Gazing 143
- 9.5 Benefits of Nasikagra Drishti (Nose-Tip gazing) 144
- 9.6 Chinese Meridians and Nasikagra Drishti Mudra 145

Chapter 10: Trataka on Thumb (Thumb–Gazing) 147

- 10.1 Trataka on Thumb 147
- 10.2 Technique of Thumb Gazing 147

| 10.3 | When to avoid doing Trataka (Contraindications)? | 149 |

10.4 Benefits of Thumb Gazing 149

Chapter 11: Dakshinajatru and Vamajatru Trataka (Gazing on Right and Left Shoulders) 151

| 11.1 | Dakshinajatru Trataka (Right-Shoulder Gaze) | 151 |
| 11.2 | Vamajatru Trataka (Left-Shoulder Gaze) | 153 |

Chapter 12: Trataka on Self-Reflection in Mirror (Mirror–Gazing) 155

12.1	Trataka on Image of Self-Reflection in Mirror: (Mirror-Gazing)	155
12.2	What makes Mirror Gazing different from other Forms of Trataka?	155
12.3	Some potential Benefits of Mirror-Gazing	156
12.4	Authenticity and Emotional Awareness	157
12.5	How to do Mirror-Gazing?	158

Chapter 13: Trataka on Nabhi (Manipura Chakra): Mirror–Gazing 161

| 13.1 | Trataka on Nabhi (Manipura Chakra): Navel Gazing | 161 |
| 13.2 | Navel-Gazing in different Traditions | 165 |

Chapter 14: Bindu Trataka (Gazing at a Point or Dot) 167

14.1 Bindu Trataka (Gazing at a Point or Dot) 167

14.2 What is Bindu-Trataka Meditation? 167

14.3 How to Practice Bindu-Trataka Meditation? 168

14.4 Interesting Facts about Bindu-Trataka Meditation 171

14.5 Benefits of Bindu Trataka 172

Chapter 15: Trataka on Aum (Om) Symbol 173

15.1 Primordial, Perennial, Universal (Aum) 'Om': Introduction 173

15.2 'Om' is Primordial 175

15.3 'Om' is Apaurusheya 176

15.4 'Om' is Perennial 176

15.5 'Om' is Universal 177

15.6 'Om' in Ancient Texts 177

15.7 'Om' in Hinduism 178

15.8 Four States of Aum (Om) 189

15.9 Bindu Trataka on the Symbol of AUM 191

Chapter 16: Trataka on Sri Yantra 195

16.1 Trataka: Meditation on the Form of Sri Yantra 195

16.2 How to do Trataka Meditation with Shri Yantra? 197

16.3 Benefits of Trataka Meditation with Shri Yantra 200

Chapter 17: Trataka on Image of Guru or Deity (Murti-Trataka) 201

17.1 Trataka on Guru Murti 201

17.3 Miracles of Guru-Murti Trataka Meditation 205

17.4 Story of Eklavya as Guru's Statue Trataka Practice 205

17.5 Trataka on Deity (Ishta Devata) 208

Chapter 18: Research on Trataka and its Benefits 211

18.1 Trataka in Ayurveda for Curing Sleep Disorders 211

18.2 Effect of Trataka on Pulse Rate of College-Level Male Students 215

18.3 Effect of Trataka on Critical Flicker Fusion (CFF) and Cognitive Performance 216

18.4 Effect of trataka on the Visual Perception of Elderly People 218

18.5 Effect of Prandharana and Trataka on Orientation Ability of Physical Education Students 219

18.6	A Comparative Clinical Study to evaluate the efficacy of Jyoti Trataka and Eye exercises in the management of Prathama Patalagata Timira w.s.r. to simple Myopia	220
18.7	Changes in Heart Rate Variability Following Trataka	222
18.8	Unfolding Chakras by Trataka	223
18.9	Attaining Siddhi (Mystical Powers) by Trataka	227
18.10	Use of Trataka on the Crowd	229
18.11	Changing Negative Thoughts by Trataka	231

Bibliography *233*

Preface

Dear Readers,

I am extremely happy to see this book titled, **"Trataka: A Concentrated Gazing Technique for Mystical Powers"** in your hands. It is my firm belief that you have chosen to read this book with a specific aim in mind, and I assure you that you will not be disappointed.

The book consists of **18 chapters.**

The **first chapter** titled, "Introduction to Trataka" is an introduction and overview of Trataka. It is advised that all the readers of this book must go through in order to appreciate the rest of the book.

Next four chapters (**Chapters 2-5**) fall under the general category of 'Jyoti Trataka' trataka where this technique is practiced by receiving jyoti (light) from sun (chapter 2), moon or stars (chapter 3), candle flame (chapter 4) and fire (chapter 5).

Thereafter, in the subsequent 12 chapters (**chapters 6-17**) the trataka is practiced on form or the other. These forms are: Flower or Leaf or Tree (Chapter 6), Sea or River or Lake (Chapter 7), Eyebrow-Centre (Chapter 8), Nasikagra Drishti

(Agochari Mudra): Trataka on Nose Tip (chapter 9), Thumb (Chapter 10), Right and Left Shoulders (Chapter 11), Self-Reflection in Mirror (Chapter 12), Nabhi or 'Manipura Chakra' (Chapter 13), Point or Dot or Bindu (Chapter 14), Aum or 'Om' symbol Chapter 15), Sri Yantra, (Chapter 16), and Image of Guru or Deity (Chapter 17).

The last chapter (**chapter 18**) describes, in detail, the research work done on the Trataka techniques and their benefits.

The author sincerely believes that a book of this nature will be useful for all the readers across the globe who wish understand the significance of this Trataka (Gazing) science and practices, and get physical, mental and spiritual benefits from it.

I would gratefully and open heartedly love to receive any encouraging/critical comments as well as feedback from my dear readers at my Email ID: drjpdudeja@gmail.com

Sincerely

2022   **Prof. (Dr.) Jai Paul Dudeja**

Acknowledgements

The seeds of my interest in 'various meditation techniques' were sown more than sixty years ago by my revered parents, **Late (Dr.) Shanti Sawrup Dudeja and Late (Mrs.) Jai Devi Dudeja**. I bow to them, wherever they are in the other world.

I have greatly benefitted in going through the books and articles referred in the 'Bibliography' in this Book. I gratefully acknowledge these authors for enhancing my understanding on the subject matter of this book.

Last but not the least, my greatest admiration is reserved for **Mrs. Rita Dudeja**, **my wife**, my best friend and my constant source of inspiration, for all my ventures and endeavours like this and many others.

2022   Prof. (Dr.) Jai Paul Dudeja

CHAPTER 1

Introduction to Trataka

1.1 Trāṭaka (Concentrated Gazing) Meditation

Trāṭaka is a science that has been explored and developed by our sages, monks and ascetics. The Yogis (practitioner of yoga) have been taking birth on the holy land of this country, that's why this country has been called the land of yogis. These yogis have acquired in-depth knowledge from the gross matter to the final limit of causal world through practice and Pratyaksha Pramāṇa (direct experience of reality); such Jīvanmukta (liberated while living) yogis are Tattvagyānī (omniscient). Only such yogis have been able to fully develop their Vigyānamaya Kosha (intellectual sheath) from the beginning to the final limit to get established in the supreme knowledge and have demonstrated this truth in their lives. Their paths and methods to realize the truth may be different, but they all reach to the same state in the end.

The word trāṭaka is composed by the combination of two parts, 'tri' and 'taki' (stare). In fact, the pure word is 'Tryatak', that is, when a seeker fixes his eyes and mind on something, then that process is called tryatak; the word tryatak has been modified to trāṭak or trataka. In other words, the meaning of trāṭaka is to keep gazing at any object without blinking the eyelids. The ordinary nature of every creature is that it keeps blinking the eyelids until it is in waking state. No creature can see any object or sight uninterruptedly without blinking the eyelids so as to prevent effect of wind on the outer surface of eyes (cornea). Blinking of eyelids keep the outer layer of the eyes moist, which preserves the eyes and protects them from microscopic dust particles present in the air.

Trataka (Sanskrit: "look, gaze") is a yogic purification and a tantric method of meditation. Trataka, a technique used in a meditation practice, is one of the six purification techniques, called shatkarmas, of Hatha yoga. It involves staring at a small object, black dot or candle flame. Other objects that may be used include a dot on the wall, an object of worship, a deity, flower, rising sun, moon etc. However, a flame is believed to work best. Trataka is one of the most direct, simple and effective techniques for attaining concentration of mind. It is said to bring energy to the "third eye" (ājñā chakra) and promote various psychic abilities and mystical powers (siddhis). Traditionally, it's said that the Trataka practice allows the past, present and future to be perceived with equal clarity.

Trataka is a process of concentrating the mind and curbing its oscillating tendencies. The purpose is to make the mind completely one-pointed and to arouse inner vision. One-pointed concentration of mind is called ekagrata. There are numerous distractions which obstruct ekagrata. In fact, distraction only occurs when the senses are tuned to the external world, which means an energy leakage is occurring. Association and identification through the eyes and sight are major contributing factors to this leakage. Furthermore, the eyes constantly move either in large movements – saccades, or tremors – nystagmus. Even when the eyes are focused on an external object the view perceived is always fluctuating because of these spontaneous movements. When the same object is constantly seen, the brain becomes accustomed or 'habituated' and soon stops registering that object. Habituation coincides with an increase of alpha waves indicating diminished visual attention to the external world; when they are produced, particular areas of the brain have ceased functioning.

In trataka, the result is a 'blanking out' of visual perception, and in the wake of this suspension, the central nervous system begins to function in isolation. This experience is known by yogis as sushumna awakening. When the brain is isolated from the sense modalities and from the associated mental processes, ideas, memories, etc. triggered by these thought impressions, then the spiritual consciousness emerges. The higher brain, liberated from time and space, is experienced. Sushumna is awakened.

Trataka may also be referred to as yogic gazing in English.

Trataka is recommended in many yogic and Hindu scriptures, and there are a range of recommended methods of practicing it.

The eyelids keep blinking on their own. The task of blinking the eyelids is done by Prāṇa (subtle life force) situated in the body. The responsibility of organized activities in the physical body rests with subtle life energy. The same life element is pervading the entire universe and the physical body. This life essence is pervading everywhere in gross and subtle forms. The truth is that the entire Aparā-Prakriti (manifested transitory nature) establishes itself in Ākāśha Tattva (subtle sky element) and creates itself using Vayu Tattva (subtle wind element).

As the nature exists in three states, in the same way the bodies of all creatures also exist in three states: (i) Kāraṇa Śharīra (causal body) in causal state, (ii) Sūkshma Śharīra (subtle body) in subtle state, and (iii) Sthool Śharīra (gross body) in the gross state. The subtle body of all creatures pervades their gross body, and the causal body pervades their subtle body. The density of the subtle body is very less compared to the gross body, so the subtle body becomes pervasive within the gross body. Similarly, the density of causal body is much lesser than that of subtle body, so the causal body pervades the subtle body. The gross body is related to the gross universe, the subtle body is related to the subtle universe, and the causal body to the causal universe. Thus, the relation of every creature in gross, subtle, and causal form always remains with the macrocosm, microcosm and the causal world. Subtle and causal worlds are not visible to the gross eyes, because their density is very low.

The eyes are the windows of the soul. If that is true, how can we make use of this fact to improve our meditation practice?

Here we explore the relationship between the eyes and the brain from a scientific perspective, and then describe trataka meditation techniques to achieve stillness of mind through the use of your eyes.

Eyes, as one of the five senses, through which the mind experiences the outer, material reality, presents the graphic and visual details of this outer reality to the mind. All the five senses, gateways to the outer world, present the same reality from their individual perspectives; viz., nose: for smell, skin: for touch, tongue: for taste, ears: for sound and eyes: for sight. The mind constructs the final reality by cognitively overlapping this five-pronged information about the same entity, the outer reality.

Sight or the impressions from the eyes present the proportionally integrated elements of the outer reality in space and colour. Technically the real eye is the bundle of nerve cells known as the optic nerve situated between the retina and the brain where the actual image is constructed using the signals received by the externally visible oval-shaped eyeballs. Eyes are the most important sense organ for humans, in particular, as 80 % of the information collected from the environment, which is critical to their survival, is received through the eyes.

After the brain, the eyes are the most complex organ in the body, containing more than 200 million working parts. These are also the fastest muscle in your body, and can function at 100% at any given moment, without needing to rest. This 576-megapixel camera can distinguish over 10 million colours, and process information as quickly as the ethernet cable.

But what does all of this have to do with the mind and meditation? The relationship between eyes and the brain starts in your first days of fetus life. Your eyes start to develop just two weeks after conception, with the retina and the optic nerve developing as a direct outgrowth of

your brain. So the retina is actually a piece of the brain that has grown into the eye, and also shares a similar structure. On top of that, sight is so important that almost half of the brain is dedicated to vision and seeing.

Conventional medicine knows that the mental health conditions translate into specific eye movement patterns. That is why people with good emotional intelligence are able to read your mental state through your eyes. Indeed, there has been much research literature suggesting that the mental conditions involving attention, such as ADHD (Attention-Deficit Hyperactivity Disorder, dyslexia and anxiety, are accompanied by and increases in erratic eye movements. The same is true regarding your breathing – it changes according to the emotion or mental state you are experiencing in every moment. There is a specific breathing pattern that sets in when we are angry, for example; and another pattern when we are fearful, depressed, tired, happy, etc.

The contribution of Eastern philosophy and the "consciousness experimentation" of the Yogis is that the opposite is also true: your eyes and breathing patterns also directly influence your mental and emotional state. This is really a good news, because it is much easier to work on the level of the breathing and eyeballs, than it is on the level of the mind (which is so subtle and volatile). Next time you feel anxious, angry, or stressed, observe how is the movement of your breath, and of your eyes. Then consciously bring a sense of relaxation and stillness to them both, and you will notice that the emotional state changes as well. If you can focus your eyes, you can focus your mind.

Our eyes are constantly making microscopic jerking movements called microsaccades, designed to make sure that the image of anything falling onto the retina is constantly changing (this is called Troxler's Phenomenon). They do this so that the objects in our field of vision keep being registered by the brain; otherwise, by constantly staring at an object for long enough, it tends to disappear from our perception. In fact, our eyes can focus on multiple things every second.

This restless scan of the environment, much like our fight or flight response, was a necessity when living in the jungle. In our modern lifestyle, however, our inability to turn off this anxiety producing pattern does not contribute to our survival or quality of life. Yet, the intensive use of computer and smartphones is training us to be ever more restless with our eyes. This is one of the reasons why our attention span keeps getting shorter. Conversely, what the meditators of yore found is that by stilling these micro movements of the eyes, stillness of mind could be induced.

Interestingly, in the past few decades Western Psychology is developing theories and methodologies based on the same principle. One of them is EMDR (Eye Movement Desensitization and Reprocessing), which is a therapeutic modality for treating trauma, started in 1987 by psychologist Francine Shapiro. In a research done by the National Institute of Mental Health, EMDR was found to be substantially more efficacious than Prozac for PTSD (Post-traumatic Stress Disorder). It is now recognized as an effective treatment by the World Health Organization (WHO), and is one of the treatments for PTSD sanctioned by the Department of Veterans Affairs.

Your vision is tightly connected to your mind. Your mental/emotional states affect your eye movements. You can also affect your mind, and even manage trauma, by doing certain practices with your eyes.

1.1.1 What is the Meaning of Trataka?

Trataka means the concentrated fixation of a particular sight; it can also be put as gazing or focusing the sight on any object. The mind has an important role in what we see, the eyes only follow the thoughts, thus for doing Trataka, the mind must be trained to focus for longer intervals of time in order to keep the gaze focused on the chosen object.

Thus proper care and maintaining the hygiene of the eyes becomes imperative for every seeker for a healthy lifespan. Yoga proposes a number of techniques which describe ways of keeping the eyes healthy for as long as one lives. Practice these techniques or eye exercises consistently for a few months for availing the ensuing advantages from the same.

1.1.2 Purpose of Trataka

By fixing the gaze, the restless mind comes to a halt. Some modern people believe that the control of the ciliary (blink) reflex stimulates the pineal gland, which Kundalini Yoga identifies with the third eye. Trāṭaka is said to enhance the ability to concentrate. It increases the power of memory and brings the mind to a state of awareness, attention and focus. In short, Trataka brings mystical powers to the practitioners.

Trataka is practiced to purify vision, external as well as internal. Trataka develops profound concentration; the ability to hold and fix our attention on an object as well as to make the object disappear. Without this skill, deep meditation and ecstatic samadhi are difficult to realize.

1.1.3 Description of Trataka Objects

It includes: Sun Gazing, Moon Gazing, Candle Gazing, Gazing on Fire, Gazing in front of a Mirror, Gazing on Deity, Gazing on Guru, Gazing on the Thumb, Gazing on the Nose tip, Gazing between the Eyebrows, Gazing on the Right Shoulder, Gazing on the Left Shoulder, Gazing on a Flower, Gazing on

Sea or Lake etc. The practitioner may fix attention on a symbol or yantra, such as the Om symbol, a black dot, the image of some deity or guru, a flame, a mirror or any point, and stare at it. In candle gazing, the candle should be three to four feet (1 metre plus) away from the practitioner and the flame level with that of the eyes. Relax but keep the spine erect and remain wakeful and vigilant. The eyes begin to water. Some authorities recommend that the eyes should then be closed and then concentrate on the after-image, while others persevere with staring for 30–40 minutes. The eyes of the one who has got siddhis (mystical powers) in trataka will appear like burning charcoal in colour.

1.1.4 Here is the practice of Trataka in a nutshell:

- Sit in a comfortable posture, preferably cross-legged.
- Light a candle at a distance of about three feet in front of you.
- Ensure that the candle or any other object of focus is at your eye-level.
- Watch it unblinkingly for a minimum of ten minutes. Gradually, increase the duration.
- During the actual practice, try to be aware of your wandering thoughts and gently bring your mind back to the object.

Let us say you decide to do trāṭaka for a period of ten minutes. For those ten minutes, you must be still like a rock restricting your eye movements as well. It is important to not blink at all. Tears will start to roll down, but you should stay unmoved. Each time your mind goes off on a tangent, bring your focus back to the object. You can do trataka on any object, but doing it on a candle flame has a purifying effect on your mind.

It is best to do the practice at least twice a day: in the morning and before going to bed at night. Steadily and gradually increase your ability to stay unblinking as part of this practice. It requires patience and resolve. If you have both, you are bound to gain benefits from the practice.

1.2 Trâtaka in Hatha Yoga Pradipika

Trataka is a gazing meditation written about in the Hatha Yoga Pradipika. It is one of the classical Shat Karmas (six cleansing techniques) of Hatha Yoga. Although it is not mentioned in the classical text, this meditation is best practiced with glasses removed.

In the Hatha Yoga Pradipika the first thing we see is that Swatmarama does not worry at all about self-control and self-discipline in the form of yama and niyama. The order here is very different. It begins by saying that you should first purify the whole body – the stomach, intestines, nervous system and other systems. Therefore, shatkarma comes first, i.e. neti, dhauti, basti, kapalbhati, trataka and nauli. Dhauti, basti, neti, trataka, nauli and kapalbhati; these are known as shatkarma or the six cleansing processes. Hatha yoga begins with these practices.

There are other people who say, "Oh, I am spiritual. I don't care about the physical body; hatha yoga only makes your body-minded." What is this nonsense? When you are spiritually-minded and you sit for meditation then, when meditation is taking place, you will become aware of your body very forcibly.

You may even have to go to a doctor because you may not be able to control it. To transcend the body does not mean to just forget about it. You have to purify it. Therefore, these six kriyas of hatha yoga (neti, dhauti, basti, nauli, kapalbhati and trataka) are necessary for spiritual aspirants.

According to the Hatha Yoga Pradipika, the technique is to gaze a candle flame, the rising or setting sun while it is orange not white, the moon, a fire, a flower, the sea, an image that brings us peace...pretty much anything.

atha trāṭakam
nirīkṣhenniśchala-dṛśā sūkṣhma-lakṣhyaṃ samāhitaḥ |
aśru-sampāta-paryantamāchāryaistrāṭakaṃ smṛtam || 2.31 ||

Meaning: Being calm, one should gaze steadily at a small mark, till eyes are filled with tears. This is called Trataka by âchâryas.

mochanaṃ netra-roghāṇāṃ tandādrīṇāṃ kapāṭakam |
yatnatastrāṭakaṃ ghopyaṃ yathā hāṭaka-peṭakam || 2.32 ||

Meaning: Trâtaka destroys the eye diseases and removes sloth, etc. It should be kept secret very carefully, like a box of jewellery.

The recommended duration from the Hatha Yoga Pradipika is 15 minutes per session.

Hatha Yoga practices are alchemical practices, which can transform an ordinary body into a shining, diamond, light body. The transformation is one of perception.

There are six important preliminary practices of purification, which are referred to as the six actions, or shat karmas. These practices purify the body and prepare it to be strengthened by the practice of asana, stabilized through the practice of mudras, made calm through pratyahara, lightened through pranayama, cleared through dhyana and liberated through samadhi. The ultimate aim, Samadhi, must not be lost sight of, even while engaged in the purification practices of the shat karmas.

The body is made of our past actions, or karmas. In Hatha Yoga the term "purify" means to cleanse the ignorance, or avidya, which is the dirt that obscures the true perception of reality. True reality is not limited by external time- and space-bound objects. Yoga practices such as trataka provide the methods to transcend the limits of three-dimensional space and linear time.

The Hatha Yoga practitioner uses the purified and tuned instrument of the body in order to gain true perception of reality. Swami Muktibodhananda writes in the Bihar School commentary on the Hatha Yoga Pradipika that vision depends not only on the organs of the eyes, which are lenses or mediums for external perception but on the entire optic tracks. When you look at something, an image is projected onto the retina via the eyes, which stimulates the retina to fire impulses back to the visual cortex of the brain where an inner image is mapped out. When the image of the external object is stabilized on the retina, and held there for some time, without wavering, the image will completely disappear and along with it a suspension of normal mental processes; in other words the mind will be turned off. Complete absorption in a single object induces withdrawal from contact with the external world. In the wake of this suspension, the central nervous system begins to function in isolation, meaning without the associated mental processes of memories, ideas and intellectual concepts.

The higher brain becomes liberated from the experience of time and space. This is the awakening of sushumna naadi; the path toward Samadhi is illuminated and you can really see where you are going!

1.3 Trâtaka in Gheranda Samhita

Trataka process is treated by Maharishi Gheranda as the fifth part of total six part (Shat karma). This exercise is mainly for cleansing and purifying our eyes. At the same time it is very useful to develop our focussing power.

This is described in the First Chapter of Gheranda Samhita as follows:

> *Nimeshonmeshakam tyaktvā sukshmalakshyam nirikshayet.*
> *Patanti yavadashruni tratakam prochyate budhei. (1.54)*

Meaning:- Gaze steadily without winking at any small object, until tears begin to flow. The wise people term this process as the ***Trataka***.

Beneficial Effects of Trataka (Gheranda Samhita)

> *Evamabhyasayogena shambhavi jayate dhruvam.*
> *Netraroga vinashyanti divyadrishtih prajāyate. (1.55)*

Meaning: By practising this Yoga, Shambhavi Siddhis are achieved; and certainly all the diseases of eyes are cured, and clairvoyance is induced.

1.4 Modes of Trataka Techniques

Stilling the eyes is not the only way to achieve stillness of mind, but it is a powerful way, and the feedback is much quicker. Schools of Yoga, Zen, and Tibetan Buddhism have developed techniques based on this principle. Patanjali's Yoga Sutras declare that even in the highest state of samadhi or meditation, there are certain impressions, ideas or experiences which remain in our consciousness. Those ideas or impressions can also be experienced in the state of samadhi, and thus they disturb the concentration of mind. These deep impressions or ideas are known as pratyaya.

In Christianity the same thing (trataka) is done, although in a less obvious manner. In every church there are idols of Christ, candles and the symbolic cross. These objects act as focal points for trataka. In Tibetan Buddhism, trataka is often done on various deities, yantras and mandalas. Even Zen Buddhism utilizes trataka in the form of staring at a blank wall. So, the practice of trataka is universal and has been used throughout the ages as a method of transcending normal experience. It is very simple yet very powerful, and this is why it has been utilized by so many different systems as a means of spiritual upliftment.

Interestingly, research from neuropsychologist Marcel Kinsbourne shows that there is a definite relationship between eye position and the dominant hemisphere of your brain; so much so that changing the eye position can directly affect your mood and experience of the world. In his experiments, pictures appearing on the left side of our viewing field, and sounds in the left ear (both transmitted to the right brain), are perceived less agreeable than when they are presented to the other side. This is relevant because most of the techniques below involve holding a central gaze.

This can explain the experience of many practitioners regarding trataka meditation and similar techniques: that there is an integration and unification of the whole brain. If looking right activates the left hemisphere, and looking left activates the right hemisphere, then it's not unreasonable to conclude that holding a perfectly centred and forward gaze produces a balanced brain activity in both hemispheres.

Trataka consists of **five different modes** of practice:

1. Bahya Drishti (Outer Trataka)
2. Bahya-antar drishti (Outer and Inner Trataka combined, or Madhyama Trataka)
3. Antar drishti (Inner Trataka)
4. Shoonya Drishti (Gazing into the Void)
5. Nimntm Drishti (Continuous Gazing)

In **outer trataka**, or external gazing, the eyes remain open and focused on any steady object. Techniques of outer trataka include agochari mudra (nose tip gazing) and shambhavi mudra (eyebrow-centre gazing). This form of trataka can also be practiced by focusing the gaze on objects such as the flame of a candle, a dot, the rising sun and so on. By steadying the eyes in this manner you are automatically concentrating the mind. When outer and inner trataka are combined, first you gaze at an external point or object for some time, then you close your eyes and gaze at the after image or inner reflection of the same object. Any object can be used for concentration.

A luminous object such as a candle flame is often used by beginners because the brightness attracts the eyes and holds the gaze. It also imprints a clear image on the retina of the eyes which can be seen clearly when the eyes are closed. This inner image becomes the object of concentration during antar trataka. If it is bright and clear enough, it will hold your inner gaze so that you are aware of nothing else. This leads to concentration of the mental forces.

The method of **outer and inner trataka** combined is useful for people who are not able to develop an inner image at will, without an external counterpart. Those who can create a steady, distinct inner image without the assistance of an outer object can practice inner trataka alone. In inner trataka the awareness is focused only on an internal image. Therefore, this practice is more difficult than outer trataka alone or outer and inner trataka combined. Inner trataka is most conducive to concentration because there is no external sensory contact, as there is with the other two forms.

You should practice **inner trataka** when you are able to create a clear inner image and when your mind is reasonably tranquil and steady. If you have a vague inner image or no image and you attempt the practice of inner trataka, then you will either fall asleep or lose your awareness in the usual patterns of thought play.

Gazing into the void should be practiced after internal trataka has been mastered. This practice is also known as *shoonya drishti*. Shoonya means the 'void' or 'formless state'. It is not chidakasha. In shoonya drishti there is no object of awareness. This form of trataka is to be done with the eyes open, gazing at nothingness.

After mastering internal gazing, you can proceed to gazing into the void. Even though you could do this from the start, it is advised to first master external and internal trataka. Otherwise, your mind won't have the stability needed to make the best use of these practices, and you will likely get often lost in distraction or lethargy.

Common modalities of this type of trataka are:

- **Boochari Mudra:** Raise your hand in front of your face, and gaze at the tip of your finger for a couple of minutes. Then remove your hand, but keep gazing at that same spot. You are now gazing at space, or emptiness. Be aware of space only, and don't register any other events. When the focus dissipates, raise the hand and start again.

- **Space:** Select two objects in your visual field, and focus on the space between them. After some time, close your eyes and focus on the space between your thoughts.

- **Evening Sky:** Also a Tibetan practice called Sky Gazing (see description below).

- **Darkness:** In a lightless room, gaze at a spot in the darkness in front of you. (Warning: do not try this practice if you have suppressed emotions or were exposed to traumatic experiences, as they are likely to surface powerfully through this exercise).

- **The Seer:** With your eyes closed, turn your gaze 180 degrees around to yourself, the source of all seeing. Gaze at the "I", the observer, the perceiving consciousness. This is indeed, a type of Self-Enquiry meditation, although almost everyone attempts it without undergoing the previous training of external and internal trataka.

It takes a long time to get into this state. Your eyes are open, but you are unable to see anything because the mind has become introverted. After some time the eyes become dim. They are half open and you can see nothing. Continuous gazing is looking at any point without blinking the eyes for hours together. It is what **Ramana Maharishi** used to practice, sitting for ten, eleven or twelve hours a day, without blinking his eyes.

In trataka, the result is a 'blanking out' of visual perception, and in the wake of this suspension, the central nervous system begins to function in isolation. This experience is known by yogis as sushumna awakening. When the brain is isolated from the sense modalities and from the associated mental processes, ideas, memories, etc. triggered by these thought impressions, then the spiritual consciousness emerges. The higher brain, liberated from time and space, is experienced. Sushumna is awakened.

1.5 History of Trataka

Trāṭaka has been in use since ancient times. It may be found mentioned in scriptures and books written by several contemporary writers. India has been the land of yogis from its inception till today. Yogis also used to practise trāṭaka from time-to-time during the course of their sadhana. The yogis who used to practice trāṭaka were certainly very powerful. They not only used to perform spiritual tasks by trāṭaka, but also performed worldly tasks when required. It was done so only when there was a dire need to use trāṭaka.

Trataka is a science which has been skilfully applied since the time immemorial to the present era in the areas of warfare, spirituality and worldly affairs. Trataka is a recorded fact in the Aryan history, that an accomplished yogi can greatly mesmerise, hypnotise and control the psyche of others, by constant gazing into their eyes.

1.5.1 Trataka by Yogi Vipula

Yogi Vipula protected his master's wife from the sexual designs of Indra by constant fixation of his eyes into her eyes, thus stupefying her from advances.

1.5.2 Trataka by Yogi Vidura

The great ascetic, Vidura's act of inducing his psyche i.e. soul, into Yudhisthira at the time of his final departure, by steadily staring into his eyes, are proofs of Trataka's hypnotic powers that are as old as the Mahabharata.

1.5.3 Burning of Kamadeva to Ashes, using Trataka by Lord Shankara

It is described in the scriptures that a demon named Taarakasura, being very powerful, was creating mayhem. Being engrossed in adharma (sinful actions), the demon was humiliating the gods in various ways. He could not be slain by anybody; only the son of Mother Pārvatī incarnated from the parts of Lord Shankara and the Adi Shakti could kill him. Lord Shankara had already gone into a state of deep samādhi due to separation from His consort Sati and got established in His swarup (Self). It was necessary to wake up Lord Shankara from samādhi in order to solemnize his marriage with Pārvatī. The annihilation of Tārakāsura by the son born out of their wedlock was pre-determined. The low-spirited gods delegated the task of awakening Lord Shankara from His state of samādhi to Kāmadeva. Both Kāmadeva and his wife Rati tried to awaken Lord Shankara from His samādhi. They could not break His samādhi even after using various means.

Finally, Kāmadeva collimated an arrow on his special bow. That arrow was having a special kind of power. The arrow hit Lord Shankara in His breast due to which his samādhi got interrupted. If anyone is forcibly awakened from a deep samādhi by hurting him, he will definitely be enraged. Lord Shankara became angry as soon as His samādhi was disturbed; He understood everything within a moment. Being furious, Lord Shankara opened His third eye. The yogagni (yogic fire) emanating from His third eye burnt Kāmadeva's body to ashes, i.e. Kāmadeva became a heap of ash within a few seconds.

In this context, the most important point is that if Lord Shankara wished, He could destroy Kāmadeva with his trident or just by the power of His words, but He annihilated Kāmadeva by opening His third eye. He manifested His will power in the form of tejas from His third eye to burn Kāmadeva. It proves that the will power concentrated by trāṭaka in the form of energy becomes extremely powerful. If it is used to perform any task, the task is accomplished more quickly than using any other way. The capability of the power of trāṭaka also depends on the self-control and purity of the practitioner.

1.5.4 Repeated Use of Trataka by the King Baali

In Treta Yug (the era of Lord Rama), Baali, the king of Kishkindha, used trāṭaka several times during his lifetime. King Baali was a Kimp Purush, a species found in ancient times which became extinct; Kimp Purush are anyways very powerful. King Baali was a great tapasvi (ascetic) and a worshipper of deity Sun; he had practiced sun trāṭaka by practicing rigorous self-control. He attained proficiency in trāṭaka and was well-versed in using it. King Baali himself was very powerful and had attained perfection in the field of war. He used to cast trāṭaka on his opponent at the time of war; he used to attack on the brain of his opponent by the power emitted through trāṭaka.

In this way, he used to overpower the brain and mind of the person before him. This has impact on the subtle body. If the brain of any person is controlled subtly, then such a person will definitely become weak mentally, or the opponent will have to do as the person performing trāṭaka will wish; even if the person has immense physical power. The physical body is just like a machine, the subtle body pervaded in the subtle body actually works. By empowering the mind and brain of anybody, the person will do as the message will be sent to him, because now he is not independent, his mind and brain are controlled by someone. No one was ever ready to fight with King Baali, who was adept in the science of trāṭaka. Anyone who fought against him, was sure to suffer defeat.

There is very illuminating anecdote found in the life of King Baali. The king of Lanka, Rāvaṇa was endowed with a boon by pleasing Lord Brahma by his intense tapasya (austerities). He had learnt many demonic sciences and became very egoistic and impious. He used to harass the seers, hermits and ascetics without reason and used to create hindrance in their tapasya. Once upon a time, in the evening, he came across Baali, who was busy in worshiping the deity Sun at that time. The egoistic King Rāvaṇa began to challenge Baali at that very time. Baali tried repeatedly to explain the situation to him, but it had no effect on Rāvaṇa, who continued to challenge him again and again. Rāvaṇa thought that Baali did not want to fight due to fear. Baali got ready to fight with Rāvaṇa due to repeated challenges. Rāvaṇa did not know about Baali; as soon as Baali came before Rāvaṇa to wage war, he attacked Rāvaṇa by trāṭaka and began to fight against him. Being mentally fragile, Rāvaṇa could not stand before him. Baali defeated him and clenched him in his arms. When Rāvaṇa could not get rid of his clench, he had to implore Baali and then Baali released him.

1.5.5 Incineration of Kalayavana by Muchkunda through Trataka

Muchkunda was the son of the king Mandhata of Ikvakshu's dynasty was. At that time, the Devasur Yuddha (war between gods and demons) started. On the request of Indra, the king of gods, the illustrious king Muchkunda fought against the demons along with the gods for a long time to protect dharma (righteousness). At last, the gods won. Due to prolonged combat, king Muchkunda could not sleep. He went to a lonely cave to enjoy deep sleep after asking Indra. He went inside the cave so that no disturbance could be there in his sleep.

Then, at the end of Dwapar Yug (the era of Lord Krishna), there was a combat of Lord Krishna with Kālayavana who was a friend of Jarasandh. Shri Krishna did not kill Kālayavana, rather began to run away from the battlefield before him, because He had something else in mind. Kālayavana continued to chase running Shri Krishna. Shri Krishna entered in that cave very cleverly, with Kālayavana running after Him, where Muchkunda had already been sleeping for a prolonged time. Shri Krishna put

His pītāmbara (yellow-coloured cloth) on sleeping Muchkunda and hid aside in the cave. Kālayavana also entered the cave chasing Lord Krishna. When Kālayavana saw Muchkunda enshrouded pītāmbara in the cave, he misunderstood that Krishna is pretending to sleep covering himself with pītāmbara. Kālayavana began to wake Muchkunda under misconception of Krishna indecently. While waking him, Kālayavana behaved indecently with Muchkunda. Muchkunda, who was sleeping for a prolonged time, woke up, but his sleep was not been completed, he was awakened forcibly by Kālayavana. He became furious due to his awakening in this manner. Muchkunda saw Kālayavana and thought that he had woken him for no reason. Consequently, Muchkunda burnt him to ashes using the power of trāṭaka, by yogagni emanated from his eyes within few seconds.

1.5.6 Gandhari made the body of her son Rock-Solid by Trataka

This is an incident of Mahabhaarata, when the battle of Mahabhaarata was being fought. Kauravas were being killed one-by-one. Towards the final days of the war, when only Duryodhana was left behind, he went to his mother Gandhari at home to ask her for a boon to get victory in the battle. He prayed to his mother Gandhari, "O Mother! Please bestow me with a boon so that I may win the battle." His mother Gandhari refused to endow him with such a boon, but due to affection towards her son, she said, "I will not bestow you with such a boon, but can provide you with such a shield, which will make your body hard like a rock". Duryodhana got ready for it. Gandhari said, "First, you should bathe in Ganges and return in a naked state, I will then bless you with the shield". Duryodhana went to take bath in Ganges. While returning back after taking bath, Lord Krishna met him on the way, Shri Krishna, being omniscient, knew everything. On seeing Lord Krishna, Duryodhana hesitated a bit owing to his nudity. Shri Krishna asked, "Where are you going this time in such a state?" Duryodhana said, "I am going to my mother". Shri Krishna said, "Are you going to your mother in a naked state! Now you are not a kid, you are a young man, is it adequate to go in such a condition?" After saying this, Shri Krishna left the place. Duryodhana thought, "It's true, I should not go in such a state." After thinking a while, Duryodhana wore a small loin in the middle part of his body and reached to his mother. Duryodhana said to his mother, "O Mother! As per your

command, I came back after taking bath in the Ganges". Gandhari said, "Stand before me". Duryodhana stood before her. Gandhari invariably used to wear a strip on her eyes. She was a devotee of Lord Shankara, devoted to her husband and follower of intense discipline, so she was having yoga-bala. But due to her infatuation towards her son, she was doing all this. She removed the strip of her eyes, which was tied for several years, before Duryodhana and she made Duryodhana's body like a stone by emitting entire yoga-bala through her eyes. But the place, where Duryodhana wore a loin, remained weak or could not be hardened like stone. Thus the strategy of Lord Krishna worked.

The most important thing in this incident is that Gandhari, who had earned yogic power with her intense restraint and devotion, she used it on her unrighteous son being infatuated with attachment to him. Still her wish could not get fulfilled, because the whole body of Duryodhana could not be hardened like a rock as a whole. The experimenter should always use such powers after bearing in mind dharma-adharma, otherwise it will be considered misuse of power.

1.5.7 Use of Trataka by Veda-Vyasa

At the end of Dwapar Yug (lord Krishna's era), King Shantanu solemnized two marriages, one with Devi Ganga and the other with Matsyagandha. Devvrat (Bheeshm Pitamah) was born from Devi Ganga, he had vowed not to marry. Two sons were born from Matsyagandha — Vichitraveerya and Chitrangada. But both of them died in their early age without begetting any son. Names of the wives of Vichitraveerya were Ambika and Ambalika. There was no prince to sit on the royal throne, the mother queen called Veda-Vyāsa to beget sons to these two queens.

Veda-Vyāsa was told about everything and he got ready to do this work. First of all, Veda-Vyāsa used power of trāṭaka on Ambika, but she could not bear the magnificence of Veda-Vyāsa. That's why she closed her eyes due to fear. Veda-Vyāsa told this to the mother queen, Matsyagandha, "Mother! I just returned back after doing tapasya, that's why Ambika could not bear my magnificence. She closed her eyes, so her son will be blind". How can a blind son become a king! Therefore, second time, the mother queen sent Ambalika to Veda-Vyāsa and instructed not to behave like Ambika, there is no need to fear.

Ambalika reached near Veda-Vyāsa, when she saw him and his magnificence, she didn't close her eyes but her body turned pale. Even after been told by her mother-in-law, her corpus became pale. Veda-Vyāsa told the mother queen, "Ambalika's complexion turned pale, so the son born out to her will be suffering from diseases". The mother queen began to think, what to do. This time, she decided to send a maid and for this, she explained the maid very well. When the maid reached to Veda-Vyāsa, she didn't become frightened in any manner. She endured the lustre of Veda-Vyāsa and did not falter. Veda-Vyāsa told the mother queen, "The maid didn't became frightened, she faced my magnificence, so the son begotten by her will be knowledgeable, glorious, pious and devotee of God".

At the end of Dvāpara Yug, this incident was of special importance. Veda-Vyāsa used the power of trāṭaka in this entire incident. By using trāṭaka, he produced the very subtle blend of the five elements, by which the foetus can be developed in the womb. The five elements are manifested here. A lesson is also learnt from this incident— both the queens (Ambika and Ambalika) could not bear the radiance of Veda-Vyāsa, so one of them closed her eyes and the second one became pale due to fear. Therefore, a blind son and the second one suffering from jaundice were begotten. At the time of the birth of son, as the thoughts of the mother are, so the son will be. That's why, it is found to be written in the scriptures that mantras should be chanted during pregnancy by mother and some other methods are also prescribed.

When a yogi practises meditation for a prolonged period, after that his body is filled up with radiance. His capacity to apply shaktipāta increases much higher than earlier. This was the case during that work. Veda-Vyāsa had to go there immediately after practicing for a prolonged period. The higher the yoga-bala, more will be the ability to perform shaktipāta. All things are not possible only by the use of trāṭaka, but the yoga-bala is also important. Therefore, while doing any task by trāṭaka, it should be seen how much yoga-bala the seeker has had. The task can be accomplished only on having attained yoga-bala.

1.6 Trataka Practices from Different Traditions

(i) Sky Gazing in Tibetan Buddhism

Dzogchen, a tradition in Tibetan Buddhism, recommends the practice of sky gazing.

1. Find a high place with a good view of an expansive clear sky. (You can also lie on your back outside and try it).

2. Sit comfortably and for a few moments calm your mind with long deep slow breaths.

3. With a good posture, tilt your head slightly upward and with a noble disposition gaze without distraction or dullness into the clear expansive blue sky (best done on non-cloudy days).

4. Let go of all thoughts, allowing them to pass by like clouds, and encourage your awareness to slowly merge with the expansive blue sky.

5. Notice how inner thoughts evaporate into your inner sky-like awareness like clouds evaporating in the sky.

6. Recognize that this open and expansive experience is actually the most fundamental and natural state of your being.

7. Sustain this recognition of an open and expansive state of being for as long as possible, and return to it when you get distracted.

Unlike the Yogic practices of trataka, which emphasizes concentration, the practice above emphasizes resting in a natural state of mind (which the clear blue sky represents).

Here is another description of this practice, this one much like the last stage of practices of Yogic trataka (gazing the void):

The method of Dzogchen gazing disorientates the conceptual mind. It's very important to practice the gaze first. You have to do that in order to keep your eyes from seeking forms upon which they tend to settle.

In terms of Dzogchen, we train through the senses and the sense-fields rather than through trying to let go of thought. We learn to fix the senses. We keep the senses unmoving in relation to the external world.

(ii) Sea or River Gazing

Sit by the sea or sit by a river. Focus on the surface detail of the water, so that you saw it very clearly and crisply. You would then fix your gaze. You would achieve that by keeping your eyes from moving. The eye muscles habitually track movements by flicking backwards and forwards along the line of movement. You become aware of that darting movement, and you continually attempt to freeze it – to fix your gaze.

This is a specific of many Dzogchen practices. The impression you would receive would be like a photograph taken at a slow shutter speed. This is one of the best ways to train in fixing the gaze.

The way to train in focusing in space, in terms of Dzogchen, is to learn to feel comfortable when your eyes have no object of focus. This seems challenging at first, but it is by no means difficult.

(iii) Gazing in Zen

In Zazen meditation, we rest our gaze on the floor, about two to three feet ahead. Or while facing a wall we place the gaze about one-third from the bottom of the wall to your own height. We don't gaze at the wall, but through it, to be open to peripheral vision. You are not looking at anything, and not seeing anything, but just gazing softly. The eyes are also kept immovable and half-closed, to minimize the need for blinking. Then, you bring the attention to the breath, or to the body "just sitting".

(iv) Gazing in Other Traditions

In classical Greece, the philosophers practiced **navel-gazing (omphaloskepsis)**, as an aid to contemplation of basic principles of the cosmos and human nature.

You also find the practice of **gazing in the Orthodox Church**, where icons of saints and personages from the Bible are the only companions that monastics take with them for long periods of retreat.

In Theravada Buddhism, there is the practice of **Kasina meditation**, which also starts by gazing at an external object, and later progresses to focusing on the mental image of that object. The ten objects recommended by the Buddha for this are: earth, water, fire, wind, white, yellow, red, blue, space (or sky), bright light. We can see the strong similarities with the selection of trataka objects from the Yoga tradition – which shouldn't be surprising, since the Buddha learned meditation from Yogis of his time.

In **Taoism**, there is a **flower gazing** practice, where we keep a relaxed and receptive focus on a flower, and feel that we are drinking in the colour, shape, scent, and healing energy of the flower. They also have moon-gazing qigong practice.

In **Sufism,** there is also the internal practice of "gazing at the Beloved". "If you want to know God, then turn your face toward your friend and don't look away." – Jalaluddin Rumi

In **Jewish mysticism** (Kaballah) there is the practice of gazing at certain geometrical forms and symbols.

1.7 Benefits of Trataka

Physiologically, Trataka cures diseases of the eye such as eyestrain, headache, astigmatism, and myopia. The eyes become clear and bright and able to see the reality beyond external appearances.

Psychologically, Trataka develops clairvoyance, telepathy, and telekinesis as well as strong will power and ekagrata, meaning single pointedness, without which concentration and meditation are not possible.

Spiritually, Trataka prepares one to achieve early success in shambhavi mudra, where the physical eyes gracefully roll back and up into the head, gazing, not merely seeing, into the third eye. This is where shunyata or emptiness, arises, where one becomes delightfully enraptured in the ultimate state of Shambhu/Shiva/Cosmic Self, the transcendent reality.

A benefit of fire gazing meditation is that it is an opportunity to honour our relationship with living fire. Fire is an important element for humans to commune with. Most of us have replaced our daily dose of fire with screen time, it satisfies us in a similar way but it's artificial and arguably not beneficial. Nourishing ourselves with live fire via a candle flame or something larger stokes our Agni (our internal divine fire that brightens our ability to digest and understand). It feels good to make this a daily practice, to nourish and feed our inner fire, even if only for a moment.

To sum up, **Trataka practice:**

- Improves concentration, memory, and willpower.
- Improves visualization skills.
- Improves cognitive function.
- Cures eye diseases.
- Makes the eyes stronger, clearer, and brighter.
- Helps with insomnia.
- Clears accumulated mental/emotional complexes.
- Brings suppressed thoughts to the surface.
- Increases nervous stability.
- Calms the anxious mind.

- Balances the activity in the two hemispheres of the brain.
- Improves vision in the dark (if practiced on a candle flame).
- Soothing effect on the cranial nerves.
- Enhances self-confidence and patience.

1.8 Precautions in doing Trataka

Trataka, like other intricate yogic exercises should be learned under the direct guidance of some accomplished yoga guru; otherwise there is every possibility that eye muscles as well as the nervous system may be damaged.

Eyes should be splashed and washed with cold water immediately after the trataka practice. This will stimulate the blood supply in the eye regions.

Avoid using external eye medicine or solution after trataka. Also avoid rubbing the eyes, even if in the beginning of trataka you feel some eye strain, which would be due to adaptation to eye exercises.

Avoid doing trataka on the burning sun. For better eye health, it is advised to sit with closed eyes, facing the sun. Trataka on the sun with open eyes should be performed in the early morning and late afternoon (i.e. sunset). However, trataka on the full moon of puma-maasi is the best.

Some bodily exercises before and after trataka are necessary to revitalise the tissues and nerves.

The continuous repetition and reflection upon the symbol of Isvara i.e. Aum, during trataka practice will be very beneficial spiritually.

1.9 Vision of Purushas and Dreams

When the practice of 'looking into' is perfected, the third stage is reached in trataka. This is called the vision of the divine being. Several forms manifest themselves when one's concentration is perfected on the rays of light which fall on the particular object, whether a crystal, decoction of tea or whatever. These forms are called purushas. They are of two types, bright and dark. The dark types are shadow figures which give knowledge of past and future events.

The mind becomes very steady while performing trataka and when it is concentrated, a person sees visions. Many have had this experience when in a state of stupor. So long as one remains awake, the mental tendencies become involved in many external objects, but at the time of sleep they turn inwards and become centrifugal. In this stage people dream, these dreams being the formations of their past impressions. During the practice of trataka the mind becomes concentrated, and the aspirant begins to see dreams which correspond to the predominant thought or mental attitude.

The dreams follow the mental patterns of the aspirant and reveal themselves as a reality or as symbols. A tamasic sadhaka has perverse dreams which indicate a different meaning. A rajasic sadhaka sees symbolic dreams, while a satvic aspirant sees true visions. This is possible only when there is intensified awareness and concentrated consciousness.

Through the regular practice of Trataka the sadhaka can break the chains of visual dominance and be freed from the grip of the "seeing is believing" myth, which has bound our consciousness for thousands of lifetimes.

1.10 Trataka vs. Meditation: What's the Difference?

People often have question like what to do between trataka and meditation? Most people prefer trataka meditation and this is why it gives great result in short time. Let's discuss more about both of them and how they work.

(i) Trataka (Concentration)

When you fix your consciousness on an object and that's exactly what we call Trataka. Your total energy flows towards that time only, and you become unavailable to everything else that's concentration.

The ability to concentrate is extremely, vital for anybody craving success. And success is nothing but the entire of small things in our daily lives, such as:

- Focusing on your studies so you'll score better marks in exams.
- Completing your weekly official report for this coming Tuesday.
- Making healthier food choices to lose that last layer of stubborn fat off your waist.

No doubt, having a solid concentration helps with worldly activities.

But concentration isn't meditation because concentration takes you from the within (your core) to the surface (the world), while meditation does the precise opposite.

(ii) Meditation (Awareness)

Meditation is nothing like concentration. Instead, it's quite the opposite: where concentration ends, meditation begins. Concentration may be a dimension of the mind, whereas meditation is that the state you reach when you've transcended the mind. Otherwise you can say that the concentration is mind and Meditation is No-mind.

Meditation is that the journey from the surface (the world) to the within (your core).

In Meditation (unlike concentration, during which you're focused on a specific object), you become conscious of everything (within you and around you) simultaneously. And when it happens, you come to understand another interesting fact: you're the watcher, not the doer.

Meditation helps you grow spiritually (the inside).

Some of the Trataka techniques and their benefits mentioned in this chapter, will be discussed in detail in the following chapters of this book.

CHAPTER 2

Trataka on Sun (Sun–Gazing)

2.1 Trataka on Sun

For thousands of years, many cultures and traditions around the world have practiced sun worship and believed in the healing power of solar energy.

People consider the sun to be a powerful, life-giving celestial body. According to some, sun gazing is one method of harnessing its healing power.

As the name suggests, sun gazing is a form of meditation that involves gazing at the sun. Participants look directly at the sun, most commonly during sunrise and sunset (when it is orange in colour), to connect with and soak in its powerful energy.

Some people who practice it say it boosts their energy levels, reduces stress, and helps them feel more grounded, centred, and positive. Still, there are important precautions to keep in mind.

2.1.1 In Praise of Sun in Rig Veda, Hymn XXXVII

Rig Veda is the oldest book in the world, recorded more than five thousand years ago. Hymn XXXVII of this ancient book says the following in praise of all-powerful sun:

i. Do homage unto Varuṇa's and Mitra's Eye: offer this solemn worship to the Mighty God, Who seeth far away, the Ensign, born of Gods. Sing praises unto Sūrya, to the Son of Dyaus.

ii. May this my truthful speech guard me on every side wherever heaven and earth and days are spread abroad. All else that is in motion finds a place of rest: the waters ever flow and ever mounts the Sun.

iii. No godless man from time remotest draws thee down when thou art driving forth with winged dappled Steeds. One lustre waits upon thee moving to the cast, and, Sūrya, thou arisest with a different light.

iv. O Sūrya, with the light whereby thou scatterest gloom, and with thy ray impellest every moving thing, Keep far from us all feeble, worthless sacrifice, and drive away disease and every evil dream.

v. Sent forth thou guardest well the Universe's law, and in thy wonted way arisest free from wrath. When Sūrya, we address our prayers to thee to-day, may the Gods favour this our purpose and desire.

vi. This invocation, these our words may Heaven and Earth, and Indra and the Waters and the Maruts hear. Ne'er may we suffer want in presence of the Sun, and, living happy lives, may we attain old age.

vii. Cheerful in spirit, evermore, and keen of sight, with store of children, free from sickness and from sin, Long-living, may we look, O Sūrya, upon thee uprising day by day, thou great as Mitra is!

viii. Sūrya, may we live long and look upon thee still, thee, O Far-seeing One, bringing the glorious light, The radiant God, the spring of joy to every eye, as thou art mounting up o'er the high shining flood.

ix. Thou by whose lustre all the world of life comes forth, and by thy beams again returns unto its rest, O Sūrya with the golden hair, ascend for us day after day, still bringing purer innocence.

x. Bless us with shine, bless us with perfect daylight, bless us with cold, with fervent heat and lustre. Bestow on us, O Sūrya, varied riches, to bless us in our home and when we travel.

xi. Gods, to our living creatures of both kinds vouchsafe protection, both to bipeds and to quadrupeds, That they may drink and eat invigorating food. So grant us health and strength and perfect innocence.

xii. If by some grievous sin we have provoked the Gods, O Deities, with the tongue or thoughtlessness of heart, That guilt, O Vasus, lay upon the Evil One, on him who ever leads us into deep distress.

2.1.2 Sun Gazing History

The Sun is the biggest astronomical body in our planetary system. Its circumference is 109 times bigger than that of the earth and it can accommodate 1.3 million earths inside it. Its distance from our earth is 150 million km and it weighs 333,000 times the weight of the earth. Also, 99.8% of the weight of our planetary system is the sun's weight. The sun continuously sends out fireballs that are 50,000 km long, 9,000 km wide and reach out 200,000 km towards the earth. Due to all these magnificent powers of the sun, it is no wonder that it has inspired mankind throughout history. It has been worshipped from the earliest of times by many societies living in different parts of the world. Each civilization had a different story about it.

In ancient Egypt, the sun was worshipped as Ra. Mankind and animals were said to have come into being through his tears. The king himself was believed to be the "Son of Ra". It was also believed that on his death, the king would be re-united with his father, the sun. The pyramids were regarded as a ramp or a means of access to the sky. Additionally, Ra was believed to travel across the sky in a boat and through the underworld all night. There, in order to rise again the next morning, he had to defeat the evil Apepi. He was represented as rising from the ocean of chaos to greet the world again.

In ancient Greece and Rome, Apollo came to be associated with the sun. In Mesopotamia it was Shamash. In the Americas, the sun was also known as Inta. The Indian tribes of America have many interesting tales associated with the sun. One of the stories is as follows.

"A long time ago there lived a selfish chief who kept the sun and moon and stars for himself. The world had no light at all. At that time, there lived a raven who wanted to get the light and give it to the world. The raven changed himself into a leaf and was swallowed by the chief's daughter, who became pregnant and soon had a baby. The baby was none other than the raven. The baby could see many bundles hung about in the chief's house and started to cry for them. The chief was an indulgent grandfather and gave the child the first bundle. This was a bag of stars and the raven threw them up the chimney.

They quickly arranged themselves in the sky. The child cried again and this time his grandfather gave him a bundle, which contained the moon. Again the child threw it to the sky. Sometime later, the child started to cry again. This time the grandfather gave him the sun and the child quickly changed into a raven and flew with it out the window. This was how light came to this world."

Science has proved the need for sunlight for growth, agriculture, health and numerous other aspects of human life. Many of the myths from around the world reflect a belief in the need for sunlight in the greater scheme of things. Indian mythology too understands the role of the sun. It was worshipped as "Surya" in India in ancient times. According to Indian mythology, Surya was responsible for health and life, a reflection of what was perhaps the scientific belief of the time. Surya is one of the principal Vedic deities. He is pictured as riding across the sky on a chariot pulled by seven horses. One wonders about the analogy between seven horses and the seven colours of the visible spectrum of light. To get energy for their body, Native Indians sunbathe by standing in the sun for two hours exposing maximum parts of their body, and they don't need to eat food on those days. They sustain themselves on the "micro food" of sunlight. When clouds gather, we become gloomy. We see the sun and feel energized.

2.1.3 What is sun gazing?

The sun is the primary source of energy to the earth, and the solar energy it gives us has been revered since the earliest civilizations. It is believed that sun gazing connects us with the sun's primal power.

Sun gazing is a form of meditation that allows us to reconnect with this natural life force. In its most basic form, it involves looking at the sun and being charged by its energy, which we can then take away and harness in our day.

Sun gazing is similar to other meditative practices like moon gazing or candle gazing meditation. Sun gazing can bring on a heightened sense of inner peace and relaxation. It may even be easier than traditional meditation practices.

In some respects, sun gazing is easier than a more traditional meditation, as you have a physical visual to focus on — the sun — which will stop your mind from wandering.

We have a super computer in our bodies given to us by the nature, which is our brain. The brain is more powerful than the most advanced super computer. Each and every human being is gifted with innumerable talents, and infinite inherent powers by nature. Individuals should never underestimate themselves. Everyone is gifted. If we make use of these powers, we can take ourselves to great levels. Unfortunately, these infinite inherent powers are programmed in that part of the brain that is largely dormant and goes unused. Even medical science agrees that we hardly make use of about 5–7% of the brain. The most brilliant of humans like Albert Einstein, is reported to have used only about 32% of their brains.

If we can activate the human brain and awaken these infinite powers inherent in ourselves, we can raise ourselves to higher levels. We can achieve any results we want. In order to operate the brain effectively, it needs to be activated. Being a holistic entity it needs a holistic power supply. Sun energy is the source that powers the brain. It can enter and leave the human body or the brain only through one organ, and that is the human eye. The eyes are the Sun Energy's entry door to the human brain. They are also known as the windows of the soul. Recent research has found out that the eye has many functions other than vision. And more information continues to be revealed about the functions of the eye. The eyes are complex organs and contain 5 billion parts, much more than a spacecraft (that has about 6–7 million parts). By this, you can understand the immense capacity of the human eye.

The rainbow is in the eye, not in the sky. The seven colours of the sun are only the reflection of what is in the eye. We can create a rainbow anytime we want – go to the garden, just observe below a source of flowing water as the sun moves above. There you will see the rainbow. The eye can receive the entire spectrum of the sunlight. It's like having a glass window. The eye is the perfect instrument to receive all the colours of the rainbow. Since eyes are delicate parts of the body, we have to use them in such a way that they serve our purposes without getting damaged. Present-day teachings and ideas such as "Don't look at the sunlight at all --you will damage your eyesight," or "Never go out in the sun as you will get cancer," are causing needless hysteria and paranoia. The more you are away from the nature, the more there is a cause for illness and you will automatically support global corporations, which are bent on minting money to provide you the artificial cure. There are definite foolproof ways of getting the benefits of the nature without exposing ourselves to its adverse effects.

There is a possible scientific explanation of what may be occurring during the exercise of this sun-gazing. Since the brain is a powerful information processor and the retina and pineal gland (third eye) are equipped with photoreceptor cells, a kind of photo analysis could be taking place during the Surya Namaskar (Salutation to the Sun) that provides a person with all the energy and vitamins required for the proper functioning of their internal organs. Additionally, the rays of the sun with their seven colours contain a cure for all kinds of diseases such as Alzheimer's, Parkinson's, obesity, arthritis, osteoporosis, cancer, mental illnesses, and others.

2.2 About Hira Ratan Manek (HRM), the Famous Sun-Gazer

Hira Ratan Manek (HRM) was born on 12th of September 1937 in Bodhavad, India. He was raised in Calicut, Kerala, India, where he had his Mechanical Engineering degree from the University of Kerala. After graduation, he joined the family shipping and spice trading business and continued working there until he retired in 1992.

After he retired, he began to research and study the ancient practice of sun gazing in which he had been interested in since his childhood. This method was an old but forgotten method, which had been practiced, in the ancient times in many different parts of the world.

After working on this method for 3 years, he was able to re-discover the secrets of sun gazing. During his study, he was mainly inspired from the teachings of Lord Mahavira of Jains, who was also practicing this method two thousand and six hundred years ago. Other inspirations for sungazing came from ancient Egyptians, Greeks, and Native Americans.

Since June 18th, 1995, HRM has and continues to live only on sun energy and water. Occasionally, for hospitality and social purposes, he drinks tea, coffee and buttermilk. Until now, he had three strict fasting, during which he had just sun energy and only water and was under the control and observation of various science and medical teams.

The first of these fasting lasted for 211 days during 1995–96 in Calicut, India directed by Dr. C.K. Ramachandran, a medical expert on allopathy and ayurvedic medicine.

This was followed by a 411-day fast from 2000–2001 in Ahmedabad, India, directed by an International team of 21 medical doctors and scientists led by Dr. Sudhir Shah and Dr. K. K. Shah, the acting President of Indian Medical Association at that time. Dr. Maurie D. Pressman, MD also describes his experience with HRM in an article he wrote and later joined the team for the next observation on HRM.

After the excitement of the findings at Ahmadabad, HRM was invited to Thomas Jefferson University and University of Pennsylvania in Philadelphia where he underwent a 130-day observation period. This Science/Medical Team wanted to observe and examine his retina, pineal gland and brain; therefore this observation team was led by Dr. Andrew B. Newberg, a leading authority on the brain and this was also featured in the recent movie "What the Bleep Do We Know", and by Dr. George C. Brenard, the leading authority on the pineal gland. Initial results found that the gray cells in HRM's brain were regenerating. 700 photographs had been taken where the neurons were reported to be active and not dying. Furthermore, the pineal gland was expanding and not shrinking which is typically what happens after mid-fifties and its maximum average size is about 6 x 6 mm; however for HRM, it has been measured to be at 8 x 11 mm.

There have been many other sun-gazers who have achieved similar results and have volunteered to be tested; however due to lack of funding and other lifestyle restrictions the results have not been documented. The uniqueness of HRM is that he has surrendered his living body for observation and experiments to the scientific firmament for several extended periods of time. Although scientists and doctors have agreed that hunger is being reduced if not eliminated, due to the complexity of the various brain functions, they have not been able to explain how sun-gazing has such positive effects on the human mind or body; however more research is underway.

From 2002 onwards, HRM has been traveling all over the world to preach about the practice of sungazing so that humanity can heal their problems without any cost or guru. In 2009 HRM traveled to 80 countries in 210 days preaching and teaching this ancient solar methodology. Each year for the last few years, HRM gives on average approximately 300 lectures on sungazing in different languages. Several interviews have appeared in leading media and TV all over the world including the BBC World Services and there are several documentaries on the HRM method of sungazing exhibited on different worldwide channels to encourage the people's practice of sungazing. Additionally, many videos can be found on youtube as well as numerous links to Sungazing websites and blogs via google - in different languages such as French, Spanish, English, Hindi, etc.

2.3 Step-wise Sun-Gazing Practice for Nine Months

Sungazing is a one-time practice, usually for a period of 9 months, or 44 minutes, of sun gazing. You can break up the practice into three phases: 0 to 3 months, 3–6 months and 6–9 months. After completing the sun gazing practice, you will then walk barefoot, 45 minutes daily (if you stop at 15 or 30 minutes of sungazing, you walk barefoot for the rest of your life; if you complete the full 44 minutes of sun gazing, you walk barefoot for one year. Barefoot walking on bare earth anchors the solarized energies in your body, after which no further sun gazing or walking is required).

The practice of sun gazing entails looking at the rising or setting sun once a day, only during the safe hours. No harm will come to your eyes during the morning and evening safe hours. Safe sun gazing hours occur anytime within the one-hour window after sunrise or anytime within the 1-hr window before sunset. It is scientifically proven beyond a reasonable doubt that during these times, one is free from exposure to ultraviolet and infrared rays that are harmful to our eyes. To determine the time of sunrise or sunset, you can check the local newspaper, which also lists the UV Index as 0 during these times. Both times are good for practice - it depends on what is convenient for each individual. Sungazing also has the added advantage of producing vitamin D during the 1-hour safe period window. And if you sun gaze, the need for spectacles and their associated adjustments for the eye will go away. This method will provide better eyesight without glasses.

For those who cannot initially sun gaze during the safe periods, sunbathing is an effective method for receiving the sun energy at a slower pace until one is able to sun gaze. Best times to sunbathe is when the UV index is lower than 2. This usually occurs within the 2-hour window after sunrise or before sunset. Sun bathing during the day is to be avoided, except for during the winter months, when the UV index usually remains at 2 throughout the day, which is safe for sunbathing. Check your local newspaper to see the published results for UV Index to be sure. Also, do not use sunscreen when sunbathing during these times. When the body heats up, you perspire and perspiration is a waste product excreted by the body. When you are painted or coated with lotions and creams – they degenerate and the chemicals enter your body. It is our malpractice -our wrong use- why we blame the sun for skin cancers.

(i) 0 - 3 Months

First day, during the safe hours, look directly at the sun for a maximum of 10 seconds. Second day, gaze for 20 seconds at the rising sun, adding ten seconds every succeeding day. So at the end of 10 continuous days of sun gazing, you will be looking at the sun for 100 seconds - i.e. 1 minute and 40 seconds. Stand on bare earth with bare feet. Your eyes can blink and/or flicker. Stillness or steadiness of the eyes is not required. Do not wear any lenses or glasses while sungazing.

Why don't you watch the sun instead of the TV? The intensity of the TV is much greater than the rising or setting of the sun. If you can watch TV at close ranges for extended periods of time, you can easily watch the rising or setting sun safely. Develop a belief that the sun's rays you are receiving into your eyes are of immense benefit, and will not harm you. This will give you quicker and better results. Even without a belief component, you will get results, provided that that you follow the practice, however, it will take a longer time. On the other hand, you need not restrict any of your normal daily routines. There will be no worries.. Everyone has some sort of mental disorder, which is the biggest human problem, but these can be removed by the proper use of sunlight.

(ii) 3–6 months

Next, physical diseases will start being cured. 70 to 80% of the energy synthesized from food is taken by the brain and is used up for fueling tensions and worries. With a lack of mental tension, the brain does not require the same amount of energy as before. As you proceed in sun gazing and as your tensions decrease, the need for food intake will decrease.

When you reach 30 minutes of duration of continuously looking at the sun, you will slowly be liberated from physical disease because by then all the colours of the sun will have reached the brain through the eye. The brain regulates the flow of colour prana [life force] appropriately to the respective organs. All the internal organs are receiving an ample supply of the required colour prana. The vital organs are each dependent on a certain sun colour prana: Kidney, red; Heart yellow; Liver, green; etc. The colours reach the organs and address any deficiencies. This is how colour therapies work -- Reiki and Pranic Healing. There is a lot of information available on colour therapy. This is the process of becoming liberated from physical ailments over a six-month period. After 3–4 months, you can become cured of your physical ailments using autosuggestions: Imagining and visualizing healing your ailments while gazing at the sun. Scientific methods such as the solariums, crystals, colour bottles, natural stones, gems, all utilize sun energy, which is stored in natural stones. You can keep natural colour stones in drinking water to further hasten healing.

In solariums there is usually a platform at the height of 100 feet where 7 glass cabinets are constructed for each of the

VIBGYOR colors of the rainbow. This platform revolves around the sun the whole day and, according to the nature of the disease diagnosed, the patient is placed in the appropriate colour for healing. Similarly, glass drinking water bottles with different colours are kept in sun for 8 hours. The water gets solarized and water develops medicinal value and is used to treat different diseases.

Photosynthesis, which we misunderstand, does not in fact require chlorophyll. Only the plant kingdom needs chlorophyll. The human body can process sunlight with a different medium. Photosynthesis transforms sun energy into a usable energy format. This is how photovoltaic cells produce electricity, how water is heated, food is cooked in solar cooker, and solar batteries operate automobiles.

The eyes receive the entire spectrum of sunlight, which then is distributed to different parts of the body by the brain on a need-by-need basis. As a result, you are cured from all diseases. An intermediate food medium is avoided. As you continue gazing at the sun, energy is no longer being used up for mental impairments or physical ailments; thus its storage level increases in your body. You are your own master within 6 months.

(iii) 6 - 9 Months

Within 6 months, you will start to utilize the original form of micro food, which is our sun. Additionally, you can avoid the toxic waste that you take into your body when you eat regular food. Seven and a half months and 35 min of sun gazing is when hunger starts decreasing noticeably. The need for food intake decreases. No one needs to eat more than his or her hunger levels. Hunger comes because of the body's energy requirements, which are a must for its existence. Food is not a necessity for the body to function; only energy is. Conventionally, you are indirectly receiving sun energy while eating food, which is a by-product of sun energy. If there is no sunlight, no food can grow.

As you consume the original form of food, hunger decreases, starting to disappear eventually. By eight months, you should see hunger almost gone. For a dull or weak student or with no belief, this time period may be 9 months or 44 minutes. After that time, hunger disappears forever. All mechanisms associated with hunger-like aroma, cravings, and hunger pangs also disappear. Moreover, energy levels remain at a higher level. Having had this experience, the brain is now well-activated with sun energy. You have now become a "solar cooker."

(iv) After 9 Months

After nine months or when you reach 44-minutes, you should give up sun gazing because solar science prohibits further gazing for the sake of eye care. The body will get discharged after six days when you stop practicing, and it has to be recharged. Now the second practice you have to start is walking barefoot on bare earth for 45 minutes daily for a total of 365 days. Relaxed walking only, no need to walk briskly, jog or run. Any convenient time of the day is all right, however it is preferred to do that when the earth is warmer and sunlight is falling on your body. When you walk barefoot, an important gland in the brain's center called the pineal gland, or the third eye, is activated. The big toe of the foot represents this gland.

Many years ago pineal gland was considered a useless gland; now it has become an important gland for study and a large number of research papers have been published about it. It has always been known as the "seat of the soul." The pineal gland has optic nerve endings. The remaining four toes represent glands too – the pituitary, hypothalamus, thalamus and amygdala. The amygdale gland, for the last 2 years, has been gaining importance in medical research. It's a nucleus of the sun or cosmic energy and plays an important role in the photosynthesis of how sunlight reaches the brain through the eye. When you walk barefoot, your body weight stimulates all these 5 glands through your toes. This is strengthened by the earth heat/energy and the sun prana falling on the head or the crown chakra. The chakras are not in the spinal cord—that is an imaginary location; they are definitely in the brain. All these create a magnetic field and the body/brain recharges with the sun energy entering into you. Relax. Walk 45 minutes for one year and food will continue to be unnecessary for you. After one year of recharging, if you are satisfied with your progress, you can give up barefoot walking. A few minutes of sun energy falling on you every 3–4 days will be enough from then on.

But if you want the immune system to strengthen, then keep on barefoot walking. Also if you want memory power or intelligence to increase, continue walking. As you increase the sun's heat on your feet, the brain will activate more and more, which will result in more activity of the pineal gland. The pineal gland has certain psychic and navigational functions. Navigational means that one can fly like birds. You can develop psychic skills of telepathy, television and place your body at different places simultaneously. Science has validated human psychic functions, and medical experiments are being done to ascertain this. Different body parts and organs become purified once you stop eating due to detoxification. Different internal organs play different mechanical roles for the purposes of space travel and flight. There are other uses other than food digestion for the internal organs. All the glands have a lot of functions and can perform at optimal level via sun energy. If you are fortunate to activate the brain optimally, you surely will reach enlightenment. You can read the past, present, and future. This method can be safely used to control obesity. Almost all problems get resolved.

Historically, a lot of people have remained without food. In 1922, the Imperial Medical College in London decreed that solar rays were the ideal food for humans. However, no one revealed what their technique was. For example, Yogananda, in his book "Autobiography of a Yogi," interviewed many saints and mystics to find out the secret of their lack of eating food. The common reply was that the sun's energy entered through a secret door and reached the medulla oblongata in the brain. They did not divulge their secret. This knowledge was lost to common folk at the time.

2.4 More Benefits of Sun Gazing

There are plenty of documented benefits to sun exposure. Evidence suggests that sunlight gazing can:

- regulate hormones and circadian rhythm;
- combat fatigue and drowsiness;
- improve sleep quality;
- ease skin conditions like acne, psoriasis, and eczema;
- increase vitamin D and bone health;
- decrease risk for certain cancers.

The sun is cyclic, meaning that it rises and sets every single day. So, it is believed that connecting with this cycle can help regulate our body's own natural rhythm. Being connected to the sun and sunlight through sun gazing allows our body's circadian rhythms to function properly. When your body is in sync in this way, your metabolism is better, which is beneficial for your overall health.

There's plenty of research to suggest that sunlight plays a part in regulating melatonin, a hormone that controls your circadian rhythm and is linked to sleep.

It is also believed that sun gazing can activate the pituitary gland, a part of the endocrine system linked to the secretion of hormones. Within the eye's retina, there are photosensitive cells, which connect with our pituitary gland. When light is received by the pituitary gland, it makes the mind and body feel more balanced.

2.4.1 It improves sleep

A 2008-study found that people who were exposed to sunlight in the morning were able to fall asleep more quickly at night, and that sunlight may be effective in the treatment of sleep conditions such as insomnia.

A 2014-study found that exposure to sunlight could be an effective countermeasure for fatigue and drowsiness.

2.4.2 Effect on Skin

According to The World Health Organization (WHO), sunlight exposure may help certain skin conditions like acne, psoriasis, and eczema.

A 2008-study mentioned earlier found that vitamin D from sun exposure plays a role in building strong, healthy bones.

2.4.3 It reduces risk of some cancers

While it's important to note that excessive sun exposure can increase your risk of cancer, there's some research to suggest that moderate amounts of sunlight can actually help prevent certain cancers.

Research from 2008 found that people who lived in locations with more sun were less likely to have certain types of cancer compared with those who lived in locations with fewer daylight hours. These included: prostate cancer, ovarian cancer, colon cancer,

2.4.4 Benefits for eyes

It is believed that sun gazing can be beneficial for your eyes, if done correctly.

A 2017-study on myopia found that increased UVB (Ultra-Violet B) exposure was associated with a reduction in near-sightedness. However, there's no scientific evidence of the eye benefits of sun gazing specifically.

2.4.5 Benefits for mental health

The mental health benefits of sun exposure include:
- increased dopamine and serotonin,
- an improved mood,
- a reduction in depressive symptoms,

A 2011-study of 68 adults found that those who received the most sun exposure in the 30 days prior had the highest density of dopamine receptors in the reward regions of their brains.

Another study from 2002 found that sunlight directly impacted the turnover of serotonin in the brain.

A 2019-review connected sun exposure with a decrease in seasonal affective disorder, or depression provoked by seasonal change.

A 2021-study also found that people who enjoyed daily sunlight over a 30-day period experienced a decrease in depressive episodes.

Sun gazing can be incredibly calming. When you focus your mind and body on the sun, you'll form a deep connection with it. This energy will naturally calm your mind and encourage the sensation of clarity and focus.

Being in the sun increases levels of serotonin and dopamine, which lift our mood. The fact that this meditation takes place alfresco means we have to go outside, which is always beneficial for mental health.

2.4.6 Benefits for Spirituality

Some believe that sun gazing practices can help you:

- connect with a higher power or your spiritual self,
- recharge and increase energy,
- improve your mood,
- attract positive energy.

When we're in the meditative state of sun gazing, we can focus on our inner desires. Being able to do this can help us manifest and attract the right energies that we need in our life at that time. The spiritual benefits of sun gazing aren't documented by scientific research, however.

CHAPTER 3

Trataka on Moon or Stars (Moon- or Stars-Gazing)

3.1 Gazing at the Moon

Gazing at the Moon is an ancient tradition dating back to the Zhou Dynasty (around 500 BC) when people held ceremonies to welcome the full moon with huge outdoor feasts of moon cakes, watermelons, apricots, apples, grapes and other fresh fruits. The popularity of this ancient tradition began to grow during the Tang and Song Dynasties when high ranking people held banquets in their big courtyards.

During the celebration they drank fine wine, watched the moon and listened to music. Common people who could not afford big parties like the rich and would put some food such as moon cakes and fruit on a table in their courtyard and pray to the moon for a good harvest. This practice greatly increased during the Song Dynasty, and historical documents describe mid-autumn night in the capital, where people would flock to the night markets and together with their families admire the beauty of the full moon. There are also many classic songs and well-known verses about this tradition.

3.2 The Story of the Moon Gazing Hare

There is a history of hares being linked to the moon which is almost universal (you'll find stories of Hares and moons in Japan and China, Mexico and through Europe) and goes back to ancient times. Whether or not hares really gaze at the Moon is not really clear, but it certainly follows the moons evening progress, as an animal who is usually most active in twilight hours and certainly, we have long been fascinated by the hare - Britain's fastest land mammal, surrounded by myth and infamous for their 'mad' March courtship rituals.

The Myth of the Moon Gazing Hare reflects ancient beliefs. Pagans believed that seeing a moon gazing hare would bring growth, re-birth, and abundance, new beginnings and good fortune.

In pre-Christian times the Hare was considered a sacred animal, entwined with the earth or white Goddess who was the provider of all things.

Queen Boudicca is said to have prayed to a hare Goddess before going into battle with the Romans. the Saxons who colonized Britain worshipped a Hare goddess.

It is suggested that the Hare is symbolic of our relationship with the land and could be identified with our need to temper our use of the natural environment.

3.3 Moon-Gazing Meditation

On most nights, it's possible to look up and see one of the moon's many faces. From harvest moon to blood moon, from crescent to quarter to full, the moon remains a familiar presence in the sky. Many people consider its light somewhat special, since it has the power to brighten the darkest corners of the night. Is it any wonder, then, that cultures around the world revere the moon as sacred — even magical?

The moon plays an important role in Earth's tides, and its phases help people keep track of passing months and seasons. There are also plenty of myths and legends about the moon's power, though science has yet to find support for the more mystical among them. Still, exposure to moonlight can lead to feelings of awe and peace, along with a greater sense of connection to the universe.

Moon gazing meditation aims to harness these benefits and weave them into regular meditation for a more powerful practice.

3.3.1 What is Moon Gazing?

Moon gazing isn't anything new. Trataka (steady gazing) meditation, a key yogic technique, often involves a candle flame; however, some practitioners focus their gaze on other objects, including the moon.

When incorporated into meditation — a practice known to relieve stress and calm the mind — moon gazing may prove even more relaxing. Moon-bathing, or soaking in the light of the moon, also figures into Ayurveda, a long-standing approach to medicine in India.

3.4 Moon-Gazing or Trataka Technique

You can practice this technique as a full moon meditation or nightly, whenever the moon is available. You can also snap a picture of the moon so that you have something to gaze upon when the moon is unavailable. If gazing at the photo, you can darken the room just enough so that your focus is entirely on the photo.

There's something about the changing cycles of the moon that makes this moon gazing practice special. They remind the psyche about the cycles of life. Ultimately, all experiences of phenomena can be broken down to vibration and cycles. All matter is ultimately a collection of tiny vibrations of light.

The moon itself is a powerful meditation object because of its influence on the subtle psychic energy and dream functions. People who are very sensitive, tend to be quick to notice this.

3.4.1 How to Do the Moon Gazing Meditation?

There are two things to remember during the moon meditation. You want to breathe calmly through the nose. You also want to relax into the whole experience, allowing all tension to soften as you notice it.

Go outside to a place where you can easily see the moon.

Gaze at the moon without blinking for as long as you can. Imagine the moon as an experience happening inside of you. Ultimately, that is exactly what it is anyway.

Allow the gaze to soften so that you increase your ability to "take in" the moon. Relax into your experience of the moon. Become one with the moon.

As you become more intimate with the experience of the moon, you are, in a sense, falling in love with the moon. They become one even though they have separate personalities. This is what concentration meditation is all about.

The eyes may start to water. If so, let a few tears come out, then close your eyes. If they don't water, close your eyes once you feel like it's a strain keeping them open.

You may notice an imprint of the moon when your eyes are closed. It may be different colours than the actual moon. That's OK. You should experience some type of impression from your gazing.

This is your object of focus now.

With eyes still closed, point your eyes up toward the point between the eyebrows. You may feel a "sweet spot" that feels just right. Keep watching that impression of the moon.

The impression may start to disappear after a few moments. Open your eyes and gaze at the moon again. You have just completed one cycle.

If you don't see the impression, that's OK. Focus on your breathing during that time. When your eyes have recuperated, open them and repeat the whole cycle starting with the gazing at the moon.

Alternatively, some teachers suggest that you actually try to recreate the image of the moon when your eyes are closed. Of course, you also have the impression to work with too.

Either way, the image of the moon will reconstruct itself more completely in your mind's eye as time goes on.

The inner impression of the moon is, in a sense, just as real as the moon that you are gazing at with eyes open. Both are an experience happening inside of you. With moon gazing practice, you may become more aware of this reality over time.

If you're a beginner, you might be able to keep your eyes open without blinking for 15 seconds or so. After a while, you may increase this as stamina allows. Some people will moon gaze for ten or fifteen minutes without blinking.

The moon gazing meditation is a concentration meditation. If the mind wanders off, you go right back to the moon or its inner imprint. However, you can turn this into a mindfulness meditation as well.

When thoughts come up, take note of them and allow them to be what they are. Be the impartial observer. Focus your attention to the thinker rather than the thought. Then, gently go back to the moon.

Moon gazing meditation is fairly straightforward, particularly if you're already familiar with standard meditation.

There's no single correct way to moon gaze. What matters most is what feels right to you.

If you see the moon and it is inviting, go outside to connect, communicate, and gaze.

3.4.2 Here's a simple step-by-step approach:

- Get comfortable outside, in a safe spot where you have a clear view of the moon.
- Make sure to dress for the weather. Feeling too warm or cold can distract you from your meditation.
- If you can't get outside, find a window that lets you see the moon.

- Turn off any other lights so moonlight becomes the only source of illumination.
- Begin by closing your eyes and slowing your breath.
- Inhale slowly and deeply through your nose for a count of 3 seconds.
- Hold your breath for the same length of time, then slowly release it.
- As you exhale, imagine the moonlight washing over your body along with your breath.
- Visualize it brightening up and slowly easing any internal "darkness," such as tension or distressing thoughts.
- Continue breathing slowly and steadily as you open your eyes and gaze at the moon.
- Note its current phase and specific details that interest you: the colour, the light, or the shape of any visible features.
- Acknowledge any feelings that come up, like awe, delight, peace, or even a slight lightheadedness at the scale of the universe.
- Gaze at the moon, allowing your thoughts to flow in and out as they will. Accept these thoughts and let them pass without attempting to chase them down or pick them apart.
- Remember, the goal of meditation is increased mindfulness and inner calm, not self-criticism.

- For a more Trataka-aligned moon gazing experience, carefully relax your focus so you can stare at the moon steadily without blinking.

- Once your eyes begin to water, close them gently, then — with your eyes still closed — "look up" toward the space between your eyebrows. An internal image of the moon should appear.

- Focus on this until it fades from your mind's eye.

- Continue for anywhere from 3 to 30 minutes. Beginners may want to start with shorter sessions, while experienced meditators may opt for longer ones.

Open your eyes and consider how you feel. Peaceful? Energized? Ready to sleep? You may not notice any immediate differences, but keep in mind that the benefits of meditation tend to increase over time.

3.5 Moon-Gazing Benefits

Potential wellness benefits aside, many people find moonlight soothing. Staring up into the hills and craters outlined in the moon's glowing face might inspire feelings of wonder or fill you with a sense of calm and peace.

A budding appreciation for the moon leads you to research its power and try moon meditations.

What makes it different from other forms of meditation?

Unless you practice near a window (which is perfectly OK), moon gazing takes you out into the natural world. And time in nature can offer plenty of benefits, even at night.

Research from 2016 suggests that regular stargazers often report increased happiness, relaxation, and peace. Looking up at celestial bodies such as the moon may prompt:

- feelings of awe,
- oneness with the universe,
- a deeper sense of the greater meaning of existence.

You might even skip the traditional seated meditation in favour of standing with your bare feet on the ground. This enhances your meditation by reminding you of you connection to Earth and the cosmos. That's a vital reminder, when most of our lifestyles involve being inside, staring at screens, surrounded by manufactured material.

In short, moon gazing meditation can promote feelings of deeper connection to the universe and all things living within it.

In Ayurvedic medicine, moonlight is believed to help heal and soothe the body. The moon gently energizes, in contrast with the sun's sharp brightness. Moonlight exposure is thought to also relieve anxiety and stress and improve relaxation by prompting the natural release of melatonin. Ayurveda holds that moon-bathing (or moon gazing) may have particular benefit for females, since the moon is thought to help increase fertility and lead to more regular menstrual cycles.

Other benefits of moon-gazing include:

- improved concentration,
- better sleep,
- stronger sense of intuition.

To date, no scientific studies have explored the effects of moon gazing meditation, so there's no conclusive support for these benefits.

Some research does support benefits of Trataka meditation, however. For example:

Research from 2014 suggests it seems to help improve cognitive function in older adults.

A small 2014 study of 30 young adults suggests it may help relieve anxiety.

Trataka practitioners believe that steady gazing can help promote:

- eye strength,
- concentration,
- visualization abilities,
- improved emotional awareness.

General meditation can do a lot for you, no matter where you practice — even if that happens to be outside, gazing up at the luminous moon.

3.6 Myth vs. Fact

If you've looked into moon gazing before, you've probably encountered plenty of suggestions about what the moon's power can do. The moon is traditionally associated with fertility and new growth, for example.

In Ayurvedic medicine, moonlight is believed to help heal and soothe the body.

The moon gently energizes, in contrast with the sun's sharp brightness. Moonlight exposure is thought to also relieve anxiety and stress and improve relaxation by prompting the natural release of melatonin.

Ayurveda holds that moon-bathing (or moon gazing) may have particular benefit for females, since the moon is thought to help increase fertility and lead to more regular menstrual cycles.

3.7 Potential Risks of Moon-Gazing

Moon gazing is a low-risk way to enhance meditation, so there's no harm in giving it a try.

Looking at the moon won't damage your eyes the same way looking at the sun will. The moon simply isn't bright enough to cause harm. That said, if your eyes do begin to sting or water uncomfortably, it's probably best to take a break or blink more regularly as you gaze.

If you're concerned about night-time safety, take a flashlight and let a roommate or family member know you're stepping outside.

While meditation is generally recognized as one way to improve sleep, looking at a bright, full moon just before bed could potentially delay the onset of sleep. If you struggle to fall asleep after moon gazing, consider shifting your meditation practice to earlier in the evening.

3.8 Stars-Gazing

The practice of trāṭaka can be done at night, either by sitting or lying on the roof of the house under the open sky, because the stars will be seen at night only, when there will be no moon and it is necessary to have dark nights.

- First of all, the seeker should select such a place from where the open sky will be clearly visible. Such a place can be the roof of the house, outside the courtyard or the house where there is an open place. There may be some difficulty in choosing such a place in the city. There is no problem to find such a place in the village, such opened place will be found.

- Late night is a good time for practicing, at that time most people fall asleep and silence also remains spread.

- The seeker should lie down comfortably by laying a mat or carpet over the roof of the house, then gaze towards the sky, at that time a number of eternal bright stars are visible in the sky i.e. some stars look less bright and some look brighter.

- The seeker should see upwards by lying itself and practice by concentrating on the star that looks brighter. He should observe only that brighter star on which practice is being followed. There may be several stars of lower light shimmering around that particular star but do not pay attention on these.

- While practicing on the stars, there are no tears or burning sensation in the eyes, because the atmosphere is cold and calm.

- There is no need to practice trāṭaka on the star for a long time. Practice of 20–30 minutes is enough.

The bottom line

Plenty of people find moon- or stars-gazing restful and healing. Making a regular habit of watching them. It can boost awareness of the natural world, and add a level of wonder and peace that transcends what you might achieve with more typical meditation.

Moonlight or starlight may not impart any mystic powers upon you, but it can still promote internal peace and calm anxious thoughts — and what's more powerful than that?

Moon- or stars-gazing meditation aims to harness these benefits and weave them into regular meditation for a more powerful practice.

CHAPTER 4

Trataka on Candle Flame (Candle–Gazing)

4.1 Candle-Gazing

Have you ever spaced out, lost your phone, or forgotten why you came into a room? Had words on the tip of your tongue or been moving so quickly that you goofed? What if these moments are an opportunity to check in with your current ability to concentrate, be mindful, and adjust your life pace?

There is a practice that can bring you back to centre. Candle Gazing Meditation, or trataka in Sanskrit, means "to look" or "to gaze." The practice asks us to look "intently with an unwavering gaze at a small point" (Hatha Yoga Pradipika). A simple technique, trataka is said to relieve mental stress, reduce anxiety, free your mind from negative thoughts, and sharpen your eyesight.

Trataka is also said to pave the way for a deeper meditation practice by increasing concentration, or dharana in the Eight Limbs of Yoga. And, meditation is one of the ways we can slow down, be present, and ground our energies — especially when life is as chaotic and challenging as it is these days.

Trataka was popularized in the West by Bhagwan Shree Rajneesh (Osho), who explained the method in Dynamics of Meditation. It is a meditation technique in which we focus our gaze on a candle. Although it can be also done focusing on a yantra, a black dot, your own reflection in a mirror, a deity or guru. And in Dzogchen (traditional Buddhist teachings) it is recommended to do sky-gazing meditation.

Some believe a regular trataka practice can actually enhance your intuition, give you the ability to visualize, and deepen your spiritual connection… all things we can explore to reflect on how we show up in the world.

Trataka kriya with a candle (candle gazing) is a yoga cleansing technique (Shatkarma) used to improve vision, memory, and concentration. Trataka kriya or candle gazing can be performed as a standalone cleansing practice. It is an ancient yogic cleansing technique that is also performed before pranayama and/or meditation. It is one of the six methods mentioned in shatkarma or shatkriya. For those who are unaware, shatkarma or shatkriya refers to the six yogic purification techniques outlined in Hatha Yoga Pradipika. It is used as a purification technique to cleanse the eyes. It is also used as a supportive practice to achieve deep states of meditation by improving a yogi's ability to concentrate.

4.2 How to Practice Trataka on Candle Flame?

You need a candle and a table on which you can place it. When you have these two, follow these steps:

- Perform Trataka in a dark (not so dark) room without any breeze or draft. The flame must be absolutely steady. Breeze will disrupt your practice by causing the candle flame to flicker.

- Sit in a meditative posture. The key is to keep your spine straight and your hips at an elevated position compared to your knees.

- Place the candle on a table, adjusting the height so that the flame of the candle is at your eye level.

- Close your eyes and practice deep, rhythmic breathing for a few minutes. Your breath should be calm, even, and steady before you start. When ready, open the eyes and stare at the flame without blinking. The eyes should be slightly enlarged as you stare.

- Concentrate on the brightest part of the flame – usually towards the tip. Do not engage any thoughts that arise in the mind. Continue to gaze until tears begin to appear in your eyes.

- You can stop here. This part of the practice is called External Gazing (Bahiranga). You can continue to the next part, which is called Antaranga (Internal Gazing).

- When you close your eyes, you will see an "after-image" of the flame. Concentrate on that image, visualizing the flame to be just the way it was when your eyes were open.

- Close your eyes and concentrate on the image of the burning candle imprinted at the point between your eyebrows.

- Maintain the focus on the image until it completely fades out.

- Open your eyes and repeat the steps of from gazing the flame onwards.

- Continue the process for as long as you feel comfortable.

- End your practice by breathing deeply and feeling the bliss of your relaxed mind.

4.3 Practice Notes on Candle-Gazing

Beginner: Stare at the candle flame for 10–15 seconds and close your eyes and concentrate on the "imagined" flame for however long you can. Do it a maximum of three times per day.

Intermediate: Slowly increase the duration of staring at the candle flame. Only increase it once every three to four days. Stick to three times per day until you can start for 30 seconds.

Advanced: Eventually, you reach a point where you can look at the candle flame for 60 seconds and hold the "imagined flame" with closed eyes for four minutes. This would count as mastery of the practice. You will notice a significant improvement in concentration and vision by this point. However, do not practice this longer than the stipulated time frame as it can strain your eyes.

Antaranga trataka activates the Ajna chakra (third-eye) located between the brows. You can follow it up with Anuloma-viloma and move on to meditation. This is an excellent way to prepare for deep meditation.

Pointers to perfect the practice

- The darker the room, the better.
- Remove all rings from your fingers.
- It doesn't matter if you sit on the floor or in a chair, as long as the head, neck and spine are erect.
- Always open your eyes with a few blinks.
- **During palming,** don't let the palms touch or press the eyeballs.
- Breathe slowly and deeply, with awareness during palming.
- The facial muscles, eyebrows and eyelids should remain totally relaxed.
- Make sure the flame of the candle is as steady as possible.

4.4 Benefits of Candle-Gazing

The technique of gazing is not concerned really with the object, it is concerned with gazing itself. Because when you stare without blinking your eyes, you become focused, and the nature of the mind is to be constantly moving. If you are really gazing, not moving at all, the mind is bound to be in a difficulty.

The nature of the mind is to move from one object to another, to move constantly. If you are gazing at darkness or at light or at something else, if you are really gazing, the movement of the mind stops. Because if the mind goes on moving, your gaze will not be there; you will go on missing the object. When the mind has moved somewhere else, you will forget, you will not be able to remember what you were looking at. The object will be there physically, but for you it will have disappeared because you are not there; you have moved in thought.

If you gaze continuously at one thing, fully aware and alert … because you can gaze through dead eyes, then you can go on thinking – only eyes, dead eyes, not looking. Just with dead men's eyes you can look, but your mind will be moving. That will not be of any help. Gazing means not only your eyes, but your total mind focused through the eyes.

So whatsoever the object – it depends: if you like light, it is okay, if you can like darkness, good. Whatsoever the object, deeply it is irrelevant – the question is to stop the mind completely in your gaze, to focus it, so the inner movement, the fidgeting, stops; the inner wavering stops. You are simply looking, not doing anything. That deep looking will change you completely. It will become a meditation.

- This practice will help to relax and strengthen the muscles around the eyes by relieving nervous tension.
- The tears that are shed will clean the dirt and impurities from the eyes leaving them clear, bright and radiant.
- It also cleanses the tear glands and purifies the optical system.
- As strain from the eyes is released, you will find that a lot of anxiety and tension will be released from the mind.
- It helps those suffering from insomnia.

- The practice is a form of meditation, and if practiced continuously, it will help increase concentration and memory.

- Trataka kriya strengthens the eyes due to its cleansing and healing effects. It improves an individual's ability to visualize, which could be immensely helpful in some forms of meditation.

- Candle gazing has been used to improve memory and concentration. It is used as a shatkarma because it eradicates fatigue and lethargy, allowing the yogi to feel light, focused, and proactive.

- Trataka kriya cleanses the cerebral cortex and has a balancing effect on the nervous system. It is said to be helpful for those who suffer from sleep disorders and insomnia.

- The Hatha Yoga texts indicate that this process develops intuition by activating the Ajna chakra (third eye chakra located at the eyebrow centre. The Ajna Chakra plays an important role in our ability to distinguish between true reality and illusions. In yoga there is total emphasis on ajna chakra. Concentration on the mid-eyebrow centre is known as shambhavi mudra. It can be developed through trataka. There are also other ways. If you can handle ajna chakra properly, you can manage the different systems in the body – excretory, respiratory, nervous, coronary system and brain. You can control and manage them all. That is the precise method of yoga. Of course, asana, pranayama, mudra, bandha, meditation, concentration and relaxation are practiced but the most important point is that you

- must become the master of this command center at the pineal gland.

- Research from neuropsychologists shows that there is a scientific link between the eyes and the brain.

- **Effect of Trataka Meditation on Mental Health:** Numerous mental health conditions like ADHD and anxiety are correlated to increases in erratic eye movement.

Further Benefits of the technique include:

- Relaxation

- better mental health and enhanced concentration.

- Enhances concentration, memory, and willpower. Trataka is one of the best meditations for the style of concentration that Patanjali advocated in The Yoga Sutras.

- Heightens visualization skills.

- Clears accumulated mental/emotional issues.

- Allows suppressed thoughts to surface.

- Can reduce insomnia.

- Heightens cognitive function.

- Increases nervous stability.

- Makes eyes cleaner and stronger.

- Helps with anxiety.

- Balances brain hemispheres.

- Can help with cure of numerous diseases of the eyes.
- Enhances self-confidence.
- Increases patience.

Science is beginning to realise the benefits of candle-gazing and indeed of still-gazing in general.

The therapy known as EMDR (Eye Movement Desensitization and Reprocessing) has been used since 1987 to help cure problems such as trauma and PTSD. In one study by the National Institute of Mental Health, EMDR it was found to treat PTSD more effectively than medication.

In summary, we know from science and from yoga that still gazing can improve our mental health, and this is where the benefits of Candle Gazing Meditation come from.

4.5 Contraindications: Is Trataka Dangerous?

As is the case with every spiritual practice, Trataka kriya is safe to practice for adults if done correctly. It is contraindicated for those who suffer from epilepsy, schizophrenia, migraines, and eye/vision problems such as Glaucoma. It is not advisable to perform Trataka when the mind is agitated, angry, or the person is experiencing a headache.

4.6 Parting Thoughts on Candle-Gazing

Steady candle gazing helps you channel your mind by reducing the constant bombardment of images via the retina. It is one of the most rudimentary concentration-building exercises in yoga. There are dozens of techniques to attain the benefits bestowed by this practice.

CHAPTER 5

Agni Trataka (Fire-Gazing)

5.1 In Awe of Agni (Fire)

Fire has always been considered a magical element. The draw of fire has been noted since it was discovered and it has been used in magical rights and valued for its magical properties for as long as man has been affected by it. Over the years many cultures have incorporated fire into their spells and used fire to foretell the future, focus psychic powers, cleanse the spirits, burn off negative energy, and much more.

Past, Present, Future

Fire has been used for centuries to look into the life line of a person. The art of staring into the flames is called '**fire gazing**' and for many people it comes naturally. Others have to tune their vision into the flames and learn to relax to see what prophesies are held within the flames

This process is simple mind and body exercises where a person will sit in front of a fire and allow their mind to wander. Soft viewing, which is where you do not concentrate but merely absorb the sights before you, allows you to see the patterns within the fire. This can be done before a camp fire, a roaring fireplace, or a candle.

When staring at a roaring fire, the flames will often move and lick – creating an image or a story that can be understood by the viewer. With candle fire work, the nuance of the flame must be understood. If the flame waves to one side, this can be a yes or no, akin to a pendulum asking a question. The flame retreating or growing can be yes or no.

For simple questions or when direct answers are needed, candle gazing is fine. If you are seeking inspiration or more detail then it is usually better to have a large fire and time to practice long term fire gazing techniques over the course of at least an hour.

Releasing Negative Energy

Fire is an excellent tool for releasing energy because it not only helps to disperse it, but being a transformative energy, fire can transfer negative energy into something positive and useful. Allow the flame to enter your body and to burn off any overflowing excess that is not currently being utilized in a positive or meaningful way in your life. Focus your negativity back into the flame and then ask for direction from the fire to use the negative for something positive. It is a simple transference between your mind and the element of fire.

5.2 Agni Suktam in Rig Veda

Since time immemorial, people across the world have revered and worshipped fire (agni) in awe, source of energy and inspiration. Rig Veda, the most ancient text in Hinduism, records the following suktas (mantras) in praise of agni:

(i) Rig Veda - Mandala 1 - Sukta 1

Om Agnim-Iille Purohitam Yajnyasya Devam-Rtvijam |
Hotaaram Ratna-Dhaatamam ||1||

Meaning: Om, I praise Agni who is the Purohita (Priest) of the Yagya (Sacrifice) (Priest leading the Sacrifice), (as well as) its Ritvij (Priest performing Sacrifice at proper times); the Yagya which is directed towards the Devas, Who is (also) the Hotara (Priest invoking the Gods) and the bestower of Ratna (Wealth of physical, mental and spiritual plane).

(ii) Rig Veda - Mandala 1 - Sukta 2

Agnih Puurvebhir-Rssibhir-Iiddyo Nuutanair-Uta |
Sa Devaa E[Aa-I]ha Vakssati ||2||

Meaning: Agni was in former times praised by the Rishis, and (is still praised) now (at present times), (O Agni) Along with the Devas. grow in this place (i.e. bring the Devas here).

(iii) Rig Veda - Mandala 1 - Sukta 3

Agninaa Rayim-Ashnavat-Possam-Eva Dive-Dive |
Yashasam Viiravat-Tamam ||3||

Meaning: From Agni (the Rishi) indeed obtains Nourishment Day after Day (by performing Inner Yagya Day after Day), (By the Power of Agni the Rishi obtains) Glory of the most Heroic type (Glory obtained by overcoming the inner barriers during Sadhana).

(iv) Rig Veda - Mandala 1 - Sukta 4

Agne Yam Yajnyam-Adhvaram Vishvatah Paribhuur-Asi |
Sa Id-Devessu Gacchati ||4||

Meaning: O Agni, that (Inner) Yagya symbolized by performing the Adhvara (Outer Yagya), pervades the Sky all around (when it is done with an expansive heart for the welfare of all in your presence), (That) goes towards the Devas.

(v) Rig Veda - Mandala 1 - Sukta 5

Agnir-Hotaa Kavikratuh Satyash-Citrashravastamah |
Devo Devebhir-Aa Gamat ||5||

Meaning: Agni is the Hota (Invoker) who is Far-Sighted (with Wisdom) and is uniquely Famed for sticking to the Truth (i.e. Who understands the true motive behind the Yagya and give fruits accordingly), May that Deva (Agni) come here with the (other) Gods (and make the Yagya successful).

(vi) Rig Veda - Mandala 1 - Sukta 6

Yad-Angga Daashusse Tvam-Agne Bhadram Karissyasi |
Tave[a-I]t-Tat-Satyam-Anggirah ||6||

Meaning: O Agni, whichever part of the Worshipper you make Auspicious (i.e. Purify), (There) Your Truth indeed is infused, O Angira (Agni).

(vii) Rig Veda - Mandala 1 - Sukta 7

Upa Tvaa-[A]gne Dive-Dive Dossaa-Vastar-Dhiyaa Vayam |
Namo Bharanta Emasi ||7||

Meaning: Near your presence, O Agni, day-after-day, with our Intelligence clouded in darkness, we...... come, and offer you Reverential Salutations (so that our Intelligence gets Illumined).

(viii) Rig Veda - Mandala 1 - Sukta 8

Raajantam-Adhvaraannaam Gopaam-Rtasya Diidivim |
Vardhamaanam Sve Dame ||8||

Meaning: The bright (Sacrificial Fire of the) Yagyas, the Protector of the Rita (Divine Truth) are shining, ...and increasing the Illumination within our own Houses (i.e. within our own Hearts).

(ix) Rig Veda - Mandala 1 - Sukta 9

Sa Nah Pite[aa-I]va Suunave-[A]gne Suupaayano Bhava |
Sacasvaa Nah Svastaye ||9||

Meaning: O Agni, like a Father to a Son, become (easily) accessible to us, And support our Well-Being.

5.3 What is Agni Trataka (Fire-Gazing)? Benefits and Precautions

Out of Trataka methods, Agni Trataka (Fire-Gazing) is considered to be the most rewarding, though it is difficult to perform due to the following prerequisites. Any Sadhaka whose thoughts are filled with lust and sexual is not authorized to perform this trataka. He will not achieve any success in it.

(i) Technique of doing Agni Trataka

- Focus on the fire -flame ith a relaxed but consistent gaze.
- Let everything else fall out of focus.
- Keep the eyes focused on the flame and softly engaged for as long as you can.

- Resist the urge to blink. If you blink, it's ok, simply open your eyes up again and continue resisting the urge to blink.

- If you need to close your eyes and keep them closed, go right ahead. You may set a timer so you know when to close them or just close them when you feel like it.

- Once you have closed your eyes and decided to keep them closed, direct your gaze across your mind screen, chidakasha at roughly the third eye area.

- If directing the gaze inward and upward is uncomfortable, find a position for your eyes that works.

- Shift your focus to this point and observe the visual stimuli.

- Observe for about 5 minutes with eyes closed if you were gazing a fire for 15 minutes or more.

Alternative Technique of Fire-Gazing:

For doing agni trataka, it is recommended to go out of your home preferably in the middle of the night in a jungle or a lonely place and lit the fire by burning pieces of the wood. Take some extra pieces of wood along with you, which can be used whenever to fire brightness diminishes.

After lighting the fire, stand at distance 0f 4–5 feet from the fire. Keep your gaze fixed on the fire while it is on. This practice should be repeated for approximately every night for the next 30 nights continuously.

(ii) What happens during the fire trataka?

When a sadhaka performing agni trataka does this practice for one month, his eyes gets converted in colour from reddish to sparkling with spiritual power. He starts visualizing the pictures of gods, deities and many other pictures. As mentioned in Bhagavad Gita, the sadhaka is never troubled by the evil forces.

(iii) What are the benefits of performing fire trataka ?

The sadhaka of Agni trataka attains mastery over three out of five elements: Vayu, Agni and Akasha. This trataka does not have the remaining two elements, viz., earth and water.

(iv) What are the precautions to be taken while performing Agni Trataka?

As mentioned earlier, if you have lust or sexual desires. You should never do agni trataka. On should be living a satvik and disease-free life to get benefits from agni trataka. The mind should be pure and free from worries and jealousy.

CHAPTER 6

Trataka (Gazing) on Flower or Leaf or Tree

6.1 Trataka on a Flower

"People from a planet without flowers would think we must be mad with joy the whole time to have such things about us."

Iris Murdoch

"If we could see the miracle of a single flower clearly our whole life would change"

A Buddhist quote

"The earth laughs in flowers".

Ralph Waldo Emerson

Flower gazing meditation is a method of grounding oneself in the present and connecting to essential life energy and love. Various iterations of this have appeared in different cultural contexts, such as Taoist flower gazing meditation, a yogic gazing meditation known as trataka, and open-eyed Zen meditations. A yoga expert based in Switzerland, believes that "flowers also relate the strongest to our olfactory receptors, adding an extra level of stimulus to our senses. For this reason," she says, "[they] will also tend to provoke positive memories."

Flowers are symbols of life, openness, and beauty - usually present for life's biggest moments- birthdays, weddings, funerals… Flowers are not just an object to focus on, but a living being whose unique energy can be deeply healing and can help us channel our celebration of life. Flowers relate the strongest to our olfactory receptors. There is a myriad of activities and objects you can use to practice a simple meditation. Flowers are favourite meditation "object". Actually, calling them 'object' is an understatement. Flowers are a living being with healing energy. There is always something inherently relaxing about staring at them.

When choosing your flower to meditate on, there is, however, a couple of things to consider:

- It should be big enough, so you do not have to strain your eyes to study its details.
- It should be small enough, so it is easy to see without having to move your head.

Given their symbolic power, it's not much of a surprise that these colorful plants have come to embody the spirit of life, which is why they are a focus of an ancient form of conscious relaxation known as "Flower Gazing".

Examining a flower to see what it actually looks like, with all of its unique shapes and curves, textures, and colours is a simple and effective mindfulness practice.

6.2 How To Practice Flower-Gazing Meditation?

If you have a garden, or a flower box, or flowers in your house, allow your gaze to fall on one of them. It's good to focus on one single flower instead of a bunch. If you don't have any flowers nearby, a picture is fine.

Be sure to choose a flower that resonates with you. Set yourself in front of you at a comfortable angle, preferably at eye level. For beginners, it's better to focus on one single flower instead of a bouquet. Feel conscious of your body's contact with the ground. Connect with the earth that grew the flower sitting before you.

Touching and Feeling

- Reach out and touch the flowers, stems, and leaves. Take your time to discover how the flowers feel… Explore the softness of the flowers and the feel of the stems and leaves. Discover their moistness, noticing the variety of textures.

- Investigate the physical sensations of touching the bouquet of flowers. Run your fingers through the bouquet and listen to the sound of touching them… Allow the sense of touch to sink in through your fingertips and into your memory.

- Stop touching the flowers and close your eyes. Experience the sense of touch through your memory… When the memory of touch begins to fade, reach out and touch the flowers with your fingers. And then imagine touching the flowers once again.

Smell

- Bury your nose and take a full, deep breath. Let the flowers tickle your nose. Smell the
- fragrance and the freshness of the flowers. Enjoy.
- Remember how the flowers smell and recreate the aroma in your imagination. Keep practicing until you are able to imagine the scent of the flowers from memory.

Thoughts and Feelings

- Sit quietly and reflect upon the magnificence of the flowers. Open yourself up for new insights and realizations.

Integration

- Relax, close your eyes, and imagine looking at a glorious bouquet of flowers… You may imagine any kind of flower you wish… roses… daisies… mums… baby's breath… marigolds… bird of paradise… any type of flowers you wish.
- See the radiant colours… the rich reds… luscious yellows… deep purples… pure whites …soft pinks… gorgeous oranges… all the shades of green.

The Process of Flower Gazing

- Place yourself about a couple of feet away from the flower, and feel conscious of your body's contact with the ground. Connect with the earth and the sunshine that grew the flower sitting before you.

- Gaze at it with soft, relaxed eyes. Blink normally, smile softly and relax your facial muscles. You can meditate for as long as you like, a couple of minutes or as long as you like.

- Look at it as if it's the first time you've ever seen a flower. Discover what it really looks like. Avoid labelling what you're looking at; instead of focusing on "petals" or "pollen", see the unique shapes, colours, textures, and notice any scents in front of you. Feel its vibrant life energy. When thoughts come up, notice them, and gently redirect your attention to the flower in front of you, neither pushing them away nor indulging them.

- Practice 'kaya sthairyam' or body stillness by sitting comfortably. Sit up tall. You can cross your legs, and rest your hands (facing down) on knees.

- Gently close your eyes, and relax your facial muscles.

- Do some breathing work to stabilize the mind: as you inhale, roll your shoulders up to your ears, and as you exhale, drop your shoulders down. Repeat three times.

- Once the mind is present, gently open your eyes, and gaze at the flower, and study it. Notice its unique shape, contours, colours, texture and scent present in front of you.

- Close your eyes halfway, and see how long you can focus on the flower without blinking or closing eyes all the way. Fixing the gaze helps anchor the mind.

- When you feel the need to blink, gently close your eyes, and imagine the flower that you were just concentrating on. See how well you can remember details of the flower. Capture a picture of the flower in your mind, and focus on it.

- The picture you just captured in your mind might fade away. When this happens, you need to recall details of the flower. Gently open your eyes again, and re-study the flower in front of you.

After many minutes, thank the flower and offer it gratitude for its gifts. Close your eyes for a minute or so. See if you can still see its image in your mind, or feel its presence in front of you.

Continue with the rest of your day and see if you feel calmer, more relaxed, and your attention is clearer. If you start practicing this regularly, you just might start noticing the specific details and beauty not just in flowers, but in every common object you come across.

This meditation practice can be done daily for approximately 10 minutes each session.

Those who engage with nature are more likely to take an active role in helping protect it.

6.3 Dwelling in the Lotus Heart: A Meditation Practice

By visualizing your heart as a lotus flower, you can begin to create a safe, comfortable place for your mind to settle.

In yoga and meditation, the heart can be visualized as a lotus flower unfolding at the centre of the chest. Like a lotus that contracts and opens according to the light, our spiritual heart can be awakened through various yoga practices from asana practice to Pranayama, chanting, and meditation.

The following meditation focuses the awareness on the seat of one's lotus heart. For some, this will be a very natural sanctum to rest the awareness. Others may observe that the restless nature of the mind does not subside so easily. This meditation serves two purposes: First, to learn to focus the mind on any object as an internal seat, and second, to receive the healing benefits of being connected to the heart as a place of unconditional love.

To begin, find a comfortable posture for meditation (seated on a cushion or blanket, in a chair, or against a wall). You may find it helpful to set a timer for 10, 20, or 30 minutes so you can deepen your meditation without wondering about the time. You may also want to gently ring a bell at the beginning and end of your meditation.

Place your hands on your knees in Jnana Mudra (index and thumb touching), with palms facing up to open your awareness or palms facing down to calm the mind. Scan your body and relax any tension. Let your spine rise from the base of the pelvis. Draw your chin slightly down and let the back of your neck lengthen. Now plant the seeds for meditating on the lotus of the heart.

6.3.1 Meditation Practice

Step 1: Begin by quietly reading this passage from the Upanishads:

> "Bright but hidden, the Self dwells in the heart.
> Everything that moves, breathes, opens, and closes lives in the Self-the source of love.
> Realize the Self hidden in the heart and cut asunder the knot of ignorance here and now."
>
> *– The Upanishads*

Step 2: As you inhale, draw your awareness from the base of the pelvis to the centre of the chest. As you exhale, concentrate on the sensations that you feel in your chest. Stay with those sensations and allow your awareness to deepen. Do you feel heat, tingling, lightness, density, tightness? As you inhale, breathe into your heart.

Step 3: Begin to visualize a lotus flower inside your chest that is gently spreading its petals open with each inhalation. And as you exhale, just dwell inside the lotus flower.

Step 4: You may choose to stay with visualization of the lotus or you may focus on the sensation of an expanding heart. When feelings arise, allow them to pass through you like the changing light of the day, or imagine them resting on the flower like water on its petals. Dwell inside the lotus of your heart, feeling the qualities of unconditional love emerge.

Step 5: When you are ready, bring your hands together in Anjali Mudra (Salutation Seal) and complete your meditation with a moment of gratitude, reflection, or prayer to integrate the energy of your meditation into your life. You can bring your awareness to your heart anytime throughout the day to come back to the seat of unconditional love.

6.4 Trataka on Leaf

Take a large betel leaf. Prepare a collegium (paste) with castor oil and make a black dot on the betel leaf. The dot should be the size of a pea or a little smaller. Fix this leaf onto cardboard. Place a light, a lamp or a candle behind you. Practice Trataka on that dot in the morning and evening. Go on gazing at the dot continually for five or ten minutes without moving your eyelids. Do this for six months.

6.5 Trataka on Tree

Trataka on a tree is similar to all the methods adopted till now practice of trāṭaka on the nearby objects. It is necessary for the seeker to practice trāṭaka even on distant objects. Such type of practice enables the seeker to cast effect on the far away living being. To practice trāṭaka on the tree, he will have to go out of the village or of the city, only then practice can be done. It is difficult to practice trāṭaka on the tree due to the existence of high buildings of the city, but if there is a proper place in the city to practice trāṭaka on the tree, he can practice.

The practitioner should go out of the village in solitary place where there is no crowd or noise etc. The seeker should choose such a tree to practice, which is approximately at a distance of one km from him and upper edge of the tree should be pointed, because trāṭaka has to be practiced on that pointed (tip) part of the tree. He also has to see that when he is practicing trāṭaka, direct sunlight should not fall on his eyes, otherwise he will not be able to practice.

The seeker should spread his āsana and sit on it, thereafter focus his vision on the upper part of the tree at which (at the tip) he has to practice. While doing practice, he does not have to run his vision on any other part of the tree, i.e. he has not to look at the other branches excepting the tree, only the upper part of the tree has to be observed.

After few days of practice, it will appear strange in concentrating the vision on the tree, but then it will become a habit. After practicing for a few days, a yellowish colour will begin to be seen by him in the sky behind the upper part of the tree, at the place where the he is practicing

trāṭaka. During the practice, the sky is visible behind the upper part of the tree. In the beginning, the slight yellow colour spot will appear bigger, it will appear only for a few seconds and then it will disappear. This activity will continue for a few days. Then this yellow spot will be seen to the practitioner continuously. According to this practice, its colour will be change to bright light blue in future, then instead of yellow spot, the blue spherical blur will begin to appear. The seeker should continue practicing trāṭaka on tree for a long time like this.

Trāṭaka on the tree should be practiced in the morning and evening, because the light of the sun gets brighter in the sky after morning and there is a trouble while practicing in the bright light. When a spherical blue spot begins to be formed after practicing for several days, that spot is constantly visible. At that time a virtue comes in the practitioner. If the seeker tries to gaze at the sky for a few moments without practicing trāṭaka on the tree, then the blue coloured spot will surely be visible to him for a few moments, it will disappear thereafter.

Similarly, wherever he will see in the sky, the blue spherical spot will appear for a few moments. The man appears to the practitioner in the form of tejas as blue-coloured rays through the eyes. If we notice, his mind was not seen to him in this form earlier, but now with practice it is itself visible to him. The mind which was very weak earlier, but it appears to be very strong in the form of these blue rays. All this has been possible due to discipline and practice. A large blue spot will be visible to the seeker not only in the sky, but everywhere i.e. on the walls or on different substances. It will happen only when your mind will be focused on any substance or place for some time.

CHAPTER 7

Trataka on Sea or River or Lake (Jala–Trataka)

7.1 Trataka on Sea or River (Jala-Trataka)

It is difficult to do trataka on water due to the following two reasons.

The object used for doing trataka should be steady. Since water is mostly not still, it is difficult to be used for doing trataka.

Even if the water is still, because of its transparency, it amounts to doing trataka on the vessel in which the water is stored rather than the water.

When doing trataka on water, the edge of flowing water, the edge of a waterfall, ripples created by breeze on still waters, etc. are used as objects.

How to Do Jala Trataka?

7.2 How to Do Jala-Trataka?

- Sit on the side of a river bank? Or else, you can fill a vessel with water at home.

- Be seated in such a place where you can see the current of the water.

- Practice Trataka on the water, when your eyes become steady.
- Your eyes should not move; keep them on a fixed spot.
- Your eyes should not keep moving along with the waves.
- Do this practice for a few minutes and then close your eyes.
- Imagine the picture of steady water in your mind. This is known as Antar Trataka.
- Open your eyes slowly, but before that cover them with your hands without rubbing the eyes.
- Stay relaxed and still for some time before finishing your trataka practice.

7.3 Trataka Meditation on Lake

Trataka Meditation on Lake is one practice that is used to ground us in the present, and renew a sense of peace.

Instructions:

i. Imagine you are sitting on an outcrop of rock looking across at a beautiful, still lake. The colour of the lake is deep turquoise. All around the lake there are tall jagged mountains with patches of snow at the highest elevations.

ii. You focus your attention directly on the lake. The water is calm, and you can see the sharp reflection of the mountains and the trees in the motionless water.

Occasionally a bird drops down into the scene... and then you spot another... and another one. The birds dive up to the sky, flying higher and higher, until they are just dots which disappear from your sight.

iii. You focus on the sky; it is a rich blue cloudless sky; and you can trace a white pattern where a plane has flown over.

iv. You feel the sun on your face and the heat upon your body. You feel relaxed and sleepy, and totally at peace.

v. You drop your gaze to the lake, and to the large grey rocks that are heaped around the edges in uneven piles. You can see that there is moss on a few of the rocks, and occasionally a marmot appears and disappears.

vi. Suddenly you're conscious of a change in the air. A cold wind has blown in, and is gathering in strength. You notice that the sky behind you has turned leaden. You can see the trees are bending with the force of the wind. Now you feel some heavy raindrops falling on your head and legs. Also, you notice that the surface tension on the lake's disturbed. There are waves on the water - where before it had been still. Yet, it appears that the depths of the lake are undisturbed. The water makes no sound and the lake is still contained. Also, the mountains are still standing – despite the building storm. There is still a sense of peace and stability here.

vii. Apply this trataka meditation to the storms you face in life. Even when things are erupting and are threatening and angry, deep inside there is a calm you can access when you choose. That is, you know you can withdraw and can practice mindfulness.

viii. Keep sitting like this continuously looking at the lake for 15–20 minutes until your mind attains peace and calm.

ix. Now close your eyes and imagine the whole scene you have just seen with eyes open.

x. Open your eyes slowly and cup these (without rubbing) before finishing your meditation.

xi. Practice this trataka meditation for next 30 days or so and see the effects for yourself.

CHAPTER 8

Bhrumadhya Drishti (Trataka on the Middle of Eyebrows)

8.1 What is Shambhavi Mudra & Shambhavi Mahamudra Kriya (Bhrumadhya Drishti)?

Shambhavi is the name of the wife or consort of Shambhu, Shiva. In Indian mythology she is also known by various other names like Parvati, Shakti etc. It is believed that Lord Shiva had taught the technique of Shambhavi Mudra to Shambhavi told her to practice it diligently in order to attain higher awareness. Shambhu is also equated with super consciousness and it is believed that with the regular practice of Shambhavi Mudra the practitioner can make Shambhu appear before him, or realize supreme conscious state.

Another of the theories about how this gesture got its name as Shambhavi Mudra is rooted in its connect with the Kundilini Shakti which lies latent, coiled up within the Muladhara Chakra at the base of the spine as per Kundilini Yoga. As the practice of Eyebrow Centre Gazing advances with time this kundalini Shakti begins to rise upwards, piercing through the other chakras located at different locations within the spine and reaches the Ajna Chakra, located at the point between the center of the eyebrows. This point is also thought to be the seat of Shiva, or Shambhu as he is also called, and as the Kundilini Shakti reaches here it unites with the Shiva and experiences the bliss of Shambhu, thus the name Shambhavi.

The practice is also known as bhrumadhya drishti. The word bhru means eyebrow, madhya stands for in between, or center, and drishti stands for gaze. Thus, if translated to English the Sanskrit term for the practice becomes eyebrow center gazing. Shambhavi Mudra finds mention in ancient texts like Gherand Samhita, Shiva Samhita, Amnaska Yoga, and Hatha Yoga Pradipika.

In yoga there is total emphasis on ajna chakra. Concentration on the mid-eyebrow center is known as shambhavi mudra. It can be developed through trataka. There are also other ways. If you can handle ajna chakra properly, you can manage the different systems in the body – excretory, respiratory, nervous, coronary system and brain. You can control and manage them all. That is the precise method of yoga. Of course, asana, pranayama, mudra, bandha, meditation, concentration and relaxation are practiced but the most important point is that you must become the master of this command centre at the pineal gland.

The pineal gland is the guru, the master, and the pituitary gland is the disciple. This should be the relationship. As long as this relationship exists, everything is going to be alright with you. When the pineal gland becomes the disciple and the pituitary becomes the guru, then all kinds of problems beset you. Emotional problems, mental problems, psychic problems and physical problems, overactive or underactive thyroid, hyperactivity or depression of the adrenals; metabolism and catabolism are all totally out of balance. There is a state of anarchy in the body, mind and life. It is a generalized state of 'disease.' The doctor makes a diagnosis and prescribes drug after drug – antibiotics, sedatives, tranquilizers, etc. Doctors themselves do not know exactly what they are doing, or what is going on, because they consider this body to be bone, marrow, blood and flesh alone.

Chapter 1 in Gheranda Samhita describes its technique in very simple terms: Direct your eyes towards the middle of the eyebrows. Reflect on your real nature. This is Shambhavi Mudra, the most secret of all tantric scriptures. Further the same text praises this practice: The man who diligently practices and knows Shambhavi Mudra becomes Lord Shiva himself. He becomes Narayana (Vishnu), the sustainer of all and also Brahma, the creator of the universe.

It has been found that by practicing Shambhavi Mudra for a long period of time one begins to lose individual awareness and can experience higher expanded awareness. In this way, one sees the significance and essence behind everything, and realizes that one's real nature is far more than can normally be conceived. This is the reason that Shambhavi Mudra is also regarded as a meditative practice in its own right.

Earlier, the kriya was supposed to be performed only by a selected group of yoga gurus who had the experience of practicing yoga and meditation for decades. Various scriptures and text guides about yoga and meditations have explained the shambhavi mahamudra steps in detail. Some of the most famous scriptures mentioning it are gheranda Samhita, hatha yoga pradipika and shiva samhita. After thousands of years of learning shambhavi steps through these scriptures and yoga gurus, technology has made it more accessible to people.

In Yogic texts like (Hatha Yoga Pradipika: IV. 36–40) and Advayatarak Upanishad (1–8), words like lakshya, taraka yoga or simply taraka are used in place of Drishti.

The inner gaze is called antar lakshya or antar drishti while the outer gaze is called bahir lakshya.

In Hatha Yoga Pradipika (I.44), the nasal gaze (nasikagra drishti) is said to be associated with padmasana (the lotus pose), while bhrumadhya drishti (the frontal gaze) is said to be part of Siddhasana (the adept pose) (I.35)

Bhrumadhya, or the space between the eyebrows, is the location of the sixth lotus in the ascending order called the ajna chakra. It is the seat of the mind.

8.2 Shambhavi Mudra (Eyebrow-Centre Gazing)

Shambhavi Mudra (Eyebrow Centre Gazing) is an advanced yoga pose and comes under the practices of other yoga mudras. This practice is also called Bhrumadhya Drishti. In Sanskrit, the word Shambhavi is broken down into Shambhu which refers to Lord Shiva - 'the one born of peace,' and bhava is referred to as the 'divine emotion.' The name Bhrumadhya Drishti, bhru = eyebrows, madhya = centre, and drishti = gazing at a point. Thus, the practice of this mudra is done by gazing at the eyebrow point. With this kind of practice a yogi moves from external connections to internal connections. And with this connection, the yogi is absorbed in his inner experiences, while constantly focusing on his ishta devata (particular symbol), which is in most cases assigned by his/her Guru.

Shambhavi Mudra practice is mainly practiced as part of kriya yoga and for better results this is practiced along with Khechari Mudra. While gazing at the eyebrow centre, the Third Eye Chakra (Ajna Chakra) is activated, slowly taking the practitioner to a meditative state. The deeper the meditative state, sadhakas will gain more from the practice of Shambhavi Mudra. In Shambhavi Mudra the students have their eyes open while the gaze is towards the point in between the two eyebrows. Slowly with practice, and when the students are in a deeper meditative state, they naturally move into Shambhavi Mudra, and some can even close their eyes while being in this state of mudra. Although it is very important to note that all of this is done only with the guidance of a guru or an experienced yoga teacher.

Shambhavi Mudra (Eyebrow Center Gazing) included in Hatha Yoga has been mentioned in the traditional text of Gheranda Samhita. This mudra is a powerful practice and is mainly practiced to reach the higher states of consciousness - which is the union with the divine. The practitioners can be advised to do this pose in Padmasana (Lotus Pose) or in Sukhasana (Easy Pose).

8.3 How to do Eyebrow-Centre Gazing?

The below cues and yoga sequences added by yoga teachers show multiple ways to do Eyebrow Centre Gazing depending on the focus of your yoga sequence and the ability of your students.

Shambhavi mudra is a very advanced form of yoga and meditation. Unlike other forms, it will take you some time to master all the steps and finally achieve your desired goals. However, once you master it, you will realize that shambhavi mudra is only a matter of practice and now you can do all the shambhavi steps relatively easily.

Here is how you can shambhavi mahamudra steps:

Stage 1:

- Sit comfortably in any meditative posture like Sukhasana or Padmasana.

- Keep the spine and the head erect.

- Form Gyan Mudra with both the hands and place them over the knees.

- Slowly close the eyes for creating introversion and relax the body, relax the muscles of the face, shoulders, neck, and the muscles holding the eye balls.

- Breathe normally throughout the practice.

- Slowly open the eyes and fix the gaze at a point in front of you, choose the point at eye level located directly in front of you.

- Fix the position of the head here, the head will not move at all from here onwards till the end of the practice.

- Now roll the eyeballs up and inwards and fix the gaze in the centre of the eyebrows.

- Both the eyes should be able to see the two downward facing curved lines of the eyebrows merging together into a V shape right over the root of the nose.
- The place where the vortex of the V shape formed by the merging of the eyebrow curves is the approximate location of the eyebrow centre.
- In case you do not see the V shape as mentioned, it means that the eyes are not converging as required.
- Hold the gaze on the centre of the eyebrows till comfortable, if a strain is experienced then close the eyes for a few moments and relax them.
- Resume the practice after sometime, practice 10–15 rounds.

The beginners may find holding the gesture for long a bit strenuous, thus they should hold the gaze between the eyebrows for not more than 10 -15 seconds initially. Slowly the endurance capacity will increase when you can gradually increase the time you should maintain the gaze in Shambhavi Mudra.

Stage 2:

- After one has mastered the eye movement one must begin mastering coordinating the eyes movement with the breath.
- Lift up the eye balls and gaze at the centre of the eyebrows inhaling slowly throughout.
- Then slowly exhale while lowering the eyes.
- Practice 10 – 15 rounds.

Stage 3:

- After training to coordinate the eye movement with the flow of the breath begin practicing holding the Gaze in Shambhavi Mudra while performing Kumbhaka (Internal retention of breath).

- Raise the eyebrows while inhaling, hold the breath inside the lungs as in Kumbhaka pranayama or suspend the breath outside the lungs (Sunyaka) for the duration you hold the mudra for, and finally release the mudra by lowering the eyes while exhaling.

- Keep the spine and the head straight throughout the practice.

- Practice for 10–15 rounds.

Stage 4:

- Five types of visualizations can be added to Shambhavi Mudra, each generate a different experience for the practitioner. As one sequentially progresses through these stages one the image of the self is developed.

- On the other hand, these visualizations aid in concentrating the mind so that the blurring of the individual awareness can take place faster.

- In the first visualization concentrate on the entire body in the form of agni, or fire. Imagine the whole body is on fire and feel the flame and the heat along the spine and the front of the body.

- In the second visualization the image of the Sun (Surya Mandala) is visualized in the Shambhavi Mudra at the point in the center of the eyebrows.

- In the third visualization the symbol of Ajna Chakra (Chandra Mandala or Ajna Mandala) is visualized at the gazing point in Shambhavi.

- In the fourth visualization white light is imagined at the centre of the Ajna Chakra, this light is pure white light, bereft of any heat or coolness.

- The fifth visualization id of lightening within the white light so imagined in the centre of the Ajna Chakra.

- Visualizing all the levels completes one round of this stage and one must initially begin with 5 rounds and move to 10 rounds over the period of some months.

Shambhavi Mudra - Variations and Practice Note

Once one has mastered Shambhavi Mudra with open eyes one can attempt the same with eyes closed. It is difficult to maintain the mudra with closed eyes as the gaze here lack any navigation indicators, like the V shape formed by the curvatures of the eyebrows while doing it with open eyes, due to which one is prone to losing the right orientation of the eyes towards the center of the eyebrows.

In order to master Shambbhavi Mudra first practice Trataka where one is required to keep the gaze fixed on an object, and then one can gradually move to concentrating the eyes between the eyebrows as in Shambhavi.

8.4 Eyebrow-Centre-Gazing Benefits

As per Hatha Yoga Pradipika - "With internalized (one-pointed) awareness and external gaze unblinking, that verily is Shambhavi Mudra, preserved in the Vedas."

"If the yogi remains with the chitta and prana absorbed in the internal object and gaze motionless, though looking, he is not seeing, it is indeed Shambhavi Mudra. When it is given by the guru's blessing, the state of Shoonya-shoonya arises. That is the real state of Shive (consciousness)."

Bhrumadhya Drishti or fixing the gaze at the space between the eyebrows helps to arrest the movements of the mind and makes it steady in laya – a state of tranquility.

When the mind and breath are silenced together with pranayama, inside the vacuum in the ajna chakra called bhrumadhyaksha, the eyes, half-open, cease to wind and see anything. This state is called shambhavi mudra. Pranayama here refers to sustained practice of breath control.

It causes the third rudra granthi (knot of ignorance) to open up. That makes for the state of liberation (Hatha Yoga Pradipika IV; 37; IV; 74–76)

It is the huge list of benefits that has ensured that this ancient form of yoga and meditation survived thousands of years. Although almost every form of yoga and meditation has general benefits like the betterment of physical and mental, there are certain benefits that come with shambhavi mudra that are exclusive to it. Here is a list of some of the most important shambhavi mudra benefits:

It can help you transcend your mind in the shortest possible time. Although there are many other types of meditation that can help you do that, shambhavi mudra can help you do it in a short time.

Sages and yoga gurus used to go in a state of samadhi to reach a high state of consciousness. By doing shambhavi mahamudra kriya steps, you also can achieve that state without actually going into samadhi.

Our eyes are one of the most active sensory organs of our body. They give you inputs from the external world all the time when you are awake. However, when you do shambhavi mahamudra steps, you fix your eyes at one point and that helps you in focusing your thoughts on one point.

8.4.1 Physical Benefits

Strengthens and Protects: When done in a correct manner Shambhavi Mudra works on the central part of the forehead. It can thus strengthen the eye muscles and increase the eyesight and may prevent eye-related disorders like Ptosis and double vision. With longer duration of practice, sadhakas will experience watery eyes which in a way is a cleansing act, removing the toxins. Of course, this should be done only under the guidance of an experienced yoga teacher, or a guru, and the student's health condition should be kept in mind.

Brain and Functions: At the physical level the practice of Shambhavi Mudra stimulates the olfactory nerves, and the optic nerves, both originating from the forebrain. With awareness when this practice is done it increases the alpha wave production from the brain which further calms the mind and body. In this state, the brain is not processing any information which helps to reduce the stress levels, controlling anxiety to a great extent. Of course the rule of the thumb is for yoga teachers to teach this practice only if they have understood the physical and mental wellbeing of their students.

- It adds magnetism to one's personality.

- It provides anti-ageing, anti-inflammatory benefits if practiced regularly over a long period of time.

Organ and Stimulation: Scientifically, Eyebrow Centre Gazing stimulates the pineal gland and pituitary glands, which are located in the hypothalamus in the brain. These glands work together in controlling the functions of the glands with their many hormones. Gazing at the centre of the eyebrows helps bring the gap between the brain and the body, ensuring the communications between the two is smooth and free. And with regular practices, the balance between the two are achieved with the better functioning of the various organs and the glandular systems. With proper functioning of the glandular system, the body remains free of disturbances, bringing a healthy life.

Concentration and Confidence: It is said Shambhavi Mudra practices should always be done only after learning the practices of Trataka (Candle Gazing). Together they help gain better concentration, better focus, better clarity, better control over thoughts, etc. This further helps sadhakas to remain calm, yet gain confidence with their body and mind. With the regular practice of Shambhavi mudra, there arises a peaceful mind, an energetic body, and the positive vibes enhance the confidence of the students.

Therapeutic, and Healing: As this pose involves the motion of the eye muscles and focuses on the forehead, it can help prevent a migraine, headaches, irritability, tiredness, laziness, etc., that can all be part of the modern way of working, eating and living life. With guidance of course the students gain better understanding on how and where to use this mudra.

8.4.2 Spiritual Benefits

Awareness and Energy: This maha-mudra or the mighty-seal stimulates the Ajna Chakra and connects the subconscious mind to the cosmos. Done with proper guidance and with the right kind of awareness which includes breathing, the practitioner will feel a great level of energy. With focus, the alpha brain waves increase, calming the mind and further increasing the energy level in the body. This energy level helps to stay further focused, and gradually students will be able to see a steady light. Focusing on this light will help gain more awareness.

Meditation and Kundalini: The goal of any kind of meditation is to arouse the kundalini. With deep practices of meditation, the body will move naturally towards the Shambhavi Mudra (Eyebrow Centre Gazing) practice with the eyes focusing at the centre of the brows. At this stage the practitioner can awaken the dormant spiritual energy - kundalini, taking the energy from the base of the spine towards the Ajna Chakra. When this chakra is activated, the intuitive mind is heightened, developing psychic power.

Higher State of Consciousness: When the Ajna Chakra is activated with the practices of Shambhavi Mudra, it is said that the practitioners can bridge the gap between the outer and inner worlds. Through mystic experiences, the path is set to connect to the cosmic consciousness which is divine wisdom, or divine emotion. This is the ultimate goal of yoga practices, leading towards Samadhi!

As explained earlier, the practice of Shambhavi Mudra (Eyebrow Centre Gazing) is an advanced practice and should be taught only by experienced yoga teachers after understanding their sadhakas physical and emotional state of body and mind.

Effects of Shambhavi Mudra on the Meridians (Energy Channels)

The gaze and the concentration are directed to the centre of the eyebrows where, as per the theory of Chinese meridians (Energy-Channels) a very extraordinary point is located. The Chinese name for this point is Yintang, and it translates to "seal of the hall". The term seal is also used to define mudra, as the mudra seal the energy within the body and prevents it from dissipating into the external environment due to certain bodily activities.

Hall may be correlated with Chidaksha, the space where Chitta resides. Chidaksha is also the name given to the dark space one perceives when the eyes are closed. The practitioner concentrates, meditates on this space while practicing Shambhavi Mudra. As per some literature on acupuncture points within the body this is the point from where one can access and experience the inner self. Acupuncture practitioners also use this point in healing tension, headaches as stimulating this point can calm the spirit, dizziness, vertigo, hay fever, insomnia etc.

Certain points of the urinary bladder, stomach, and gall bladder meridians are located near the eye balls. These points receive stimulation was the muscles of around the eyes exhibit movement and contract while doing Shambhavi Mudra. These points are also used for the treatment of various eye disorders and the disorders of the eye muscles. A branch of the heart meridian originates from the heart, runs along the side of the oesophagus ad ends in the eye.

The eye balls movement in Shambhavi Mudra stimulates the heart through this branch of the heart meridian, as per acupuncture philosophy the heart is responsible for regulating emotions and the mind from which awareness originates. Thus, practice of Shambhavi Mudra helps calm anger, increase the level of awareness, and leads to higher states of consciousness.

As per the theory of Chinese Meridians and the related acupuncture points liver controls the eyes, it opens up in the eyes. The eye ball movements in Shambhavi Mudra influence the liver positively which enables a harmonious and stable flow of energy throughout the body creating the overall balance within.

This balancing act involves balancing of all the three doshas within the body as described by Ayurveda. It impacts the thought process and functions of the eyes positively as it balances the alochaka (critique) pitta which is located in the eye.

8.5 Precautions in doing Shambhavi Mudra

While teaching this mudra, the following precautions should be kept in mind:

Sadhakas should immediately release this mudra practice in case they feel a greater level of strain in between the eyes. Beginners may find the mudra very sensitive when they hold the pose for a longer time. So, they should restrain from the pose if they feel pain inside their retinas, or severe sensation at the center of the forehead.

Sadhakas must restrain themselves from overdoing the pose as it may cause dizziness or/and mild headaches.

Sadhakas should be advised to do the pose after removing the contact lens, or glasses, as they may cause obstacles during the practice, causing more harm than good.

Sadhakas with recent eye-surgery or brain surgery should not practice the pose, at least not without the expert's advice as it may cause more complex troubles for them further.

CHAPTER 9

Nasikagra Drishti (Agochari Mudra): Trataka on Nose Tip

9.1 Trataka on Nose Tip (Nasikagra Drishti)

Gazing on the nose tip or the nasal gaze is also known as Nasikagra Trataka. One can sit in any comfortable posture, keep the spine and the neck erect. Now fix both the eyes on the tip of the nose for one to two minutes. Repeat this multiple times by taking intervals of rest with closed eyes in between.

Nasikagra Drishti or Agochari Mudra means "Nose tip gazing". In Sanskrit, 'Nasika' means the nose and 'agra' means the end or the tip. 'Drishti' means the sight. The term comes from the Sanskrit, nasagra, meaning "nose tip," and drishti, meaning "gaze." Thus, Nasikagra Drishti literally means gazing at the tip of the nose. Nasikagra Drishti is a powerful practice to develop concentration and is used in conjunction with many meditation techniques.

Nasikagra Drishti is similar to Sambhavi Mudra in practice, except that the eyes focus on the tip of the nose, instead of the eye brow centre.

9.2 Gazing at the Nose Tip (Nasikagra Drishti or Agochari Mudra)

The purpose of gazing at the tip of the nose is to calm the disturbances and fluctuations of the mind, at the same time to balance ida and pingala, in this case to bring balance between extroversion and introversion. This is exquisitely and lucidly described in the Chinese scriptures called Tai Chin Hua Tzung Chili translated by Wilhelm: "What then is really meant by this? The expression 'tip of the nose' is very cleverly chosen. The nose must serve the eyes as a guideline. If one is not guided by the nose, either one opens the eyes too wide and looks into the distance so that the nose is not seen, or the lids shut too much so that the eyes are not seen. But when the eyes are opened too wide, one makes the mistake of directing them outwards, thereby one is easily distracted (by outer events). If they are closed too much, one makes the mistake of letting them turn inwards, thereby one easily sinks into a dreamy reverie (lost in thoughts; unawareness). Only when the eyelids are lowered properly, halfway, is the tip of the nose seen is just the right way. Therefore, it is taken as a guideline…"

There is great significance and reason behind nose tip gazing. It balances the ida and pingala and leads to awakening of sushumna. It therefore leads directly to meditation if it is perfected. This is the reason for nose tip gazing in Manduki mudra.

The purpose of specific gazes (called Drishti) in yoga is to focus the mind and bring the attention inward. Eyes open $1/10^{th}$ with the gaze at the tip of the nose is also said to connect us to the root chakra and stimulate Kundalini. It also stimulates the frontal lobe part of the brain. Yes, you will still get the benefits of the meditation if you practice with the eyes closed but the effects will definitely be heightened with the corresponding focus.

Focus at the tip of the nose with the eyes about 9/10th closed.

Symbolically, the length of the nose is taken as (is related to) the length of the spinal cord. Just as the different centres in the body are represented in the brain, the different psychic centres are also represented along the length of the nose. As at the top of the spine rests the Ajna Chakra, and at the base of the spine is located the Muladhara Chakra, at the top of the nose bridge is located the Ajna Chakra, and the lower part of the nose bridge, the nose tip is considered as Muladhara Chakra. Thus, gazing at the nose tip helps one directly activate the Kundalini Shakti located at Muladhara Chakra.

The antiquity of Naikagra Drishti Mudra, or Agochari Mudra dates back to thousands of years, as a statue of a yogi sitting with his eyes focused on the tip of his nose had been excavated from the remains of the Indus Valley Civilization, from the ruins of its site at Mohenjodaro, much before the Vedas were written. This mudra is similar to Shambhavi Mudra, where in one focuses the sight between the eyebrows, or the Ajna Chakra, in Nasikagra Drishti Mudra one needs to focus one's gaze on the nose tip instead. Both the mudras are powerful techniques for improving concentration of the mind which helps one slip into the meditative state.

Both these mudras form an integral part of Kriya yoga and must be sufficiently mastered before one begins to practice this form of yoga. Agochari Mudra or Nasikagra mudra has been mentioned in multiple ancient texts on yoga: Bhagawat

Gita, Hatha Yoga Pradipika, and the Chinese scripture Tai Chin Hua Tzung Chih. The technique appears to be too easy or simple to perform, when introduced for the first time, but takes quite a practice initially to habituate the eyes maintain the focus on the tip of the nose.

9.3 How to do Nasikagra Drishti (Nose Tip Gazing)?

Preparatory Practice

- In the beginning, it may be quite tough to focus the eyes on the nose tip. In order to overcome this, maintain your index finger up at arm's length from your eyes and focus on it.

- Slowly bring your finger towards your nose, maintaining your gaze steadily fixed upon it.

- When your finger touches the tip of your nose, your eyes should still be focused on the finger.

- Transfer the focus of your eyes to the nose tip.

- With regular practice, this method becomes superfluous and your eyes can effortlessly fix on the nose tip at will.

Practice

- Sit in any comfortable meditation posture whilst keeping your spine and head straight.

- Place your hands on the knees in either jnana or chin mudra.

- Close your eyes and relax your entire body.
- Open your eyes and focus them on your nose tip.
- Do not strain your eyes in any way.
- When your eyes are correctly focused, a double outline of the nose is observed. These two lines converge at the tip of your nose creating an inverted V-image.
- Concentrate on the apex of the V.
- Attempt to become totally absorbed in the practice to the exclusion of all other thoughts.
- After a couple of seconds, close your eyes and relax them before repeating the practice.
- Continue for up to 5 minutes.
- Do not strain the eyes. Remember to keep the gaze soft. If, at any time, you feel eyestrain, please continue with your eyes closed.
- One can increase the duration over a period of months.

Breathing

Nasikagra drishti should be carried out with normal breathing in the beginning until your eyes have adjusted to the downward gaze.

Afterwards, the practice can be incorporated with antar kumbhaka (inner retention) but not with bahir kumbhaka (external retention). When combining the practice with antar kumbhaka, your eyes should remain closed during inhalation and exhalation.

Awareness

Even though your eyes are open, the goal of this practice is to induce introspection. Your open eyes should be unaware of the outside world. Focusing them on the nose tip further concentrates the mind.

Practicing Agochari Mudra with Kumbhaka

Agochari mudra or the gesture of gazing at the nose tip is always done by retaining th breath inside the lungs - internal Kumbhaka - and not outside. The eyes are kept closed while inhaling and exhaling, the Nasikagra Drishti mudra is only maintained during the duration of internal kumbhaka.

- Begin by closing the eyes, bring your awareness on the breath at the nose tip.
- Take an inhalation while the eyes are closed.
- Retain the breath within the lungs, open the eyes slightly and focus the gaze over the tip of the nose.
- Concentrate on the vertex of the inverted V shape visible at the tip of the nose as before, retention of the breath will help intensify the concentration.
- Hold the mudra for a period which is comfortable, without any strain on the lungs or the eyes, release the mudra by exhaling and closing the eyes to relax them.
- Repeat the practice for at least 5 minutes.

Throughout the eyes remain open while practicing Nasikagra Drishti Mudra the main aim of the practice to produce introspection, with no awareness of the outside world. One should be aware of the contraction produced in the muscles of the eyes and the attention must also be kept on Muladhara Chakra.

Time of Practice

Nasikagra drishti can be carried out at any time of day even though ideally, it is best performed early in the morning or late at night just before sleep.

9.4 Contra-Indications and Further Instructions of Nose-Tip Gazing

Persons who are experiencing the following conditions as mentioned here must avoid practicing Agochari Mudra:

- Glaucoma,
- Diabetic retinopathy,
- Recent cataract surgery (practice under the guidance of a competent yoga teacher).
- Suffering from depression.

Essential Considerations and Precautions:

- Cupping of the eyes is not mandatory, will depend on the outside temperature.
- Though cupping is very beneficial after doing Trataka.
- Do not be in any hurry, blink excessively then shut the eyes for a minute in order to calm down the Mind before beginning this practice.
- Be gentle with the eyes, do not go too fast or too slow with the thumb movements.

- Consider watering of the eyes as normal.
- In case any pain is experienced in the eyes at any stage, terminate the process and close the eyes.
- Make sure that the eyes are continuously focused on the tip of the thumb.
- There is no time limit for completing one round, practice a maximum of two rounds in a single sitting, and a maximum of twice in a day.
- It can also be done while sitting in a chair.
- Children only aged 5 and above should do Trataka.
- Tears, burning sensation and involuntary blinking can be experienced after the Trataka has been done.
- A strain on the forehead or a mild headache may also be experienced as an after effect.
- Consciously keep breathing as there is a fear of getting into a suspension of breath, breathing comes naturally if the Trataka is practiced regularly.

9.5 Benefits of Nasikagra Drishti (Nose-Tip gazing)

- Nasikagra Drishti helps to develop concentration and is used as part of many meditation techniques.
- Nasikagra drishti is an extremely beneficial technique for disturbed states of mind as well as calming anger.
- It helps to strengthen the eye muscles. Initially, the eyes may pain within few seconds of practice. Later you can maintain it for hours.

- If performed with awareness for a long period, it assists in the awakening of the Muladhara chakra and induces deep meditative states.

- It also allows the practitioner to tap into the psychic and spiritual planes of consciousness.

- Nasikagra Drishti takes the practitioner to higher state of consciousness during meditation.

9.6 Chinese Meridians and Nasikagra Drishti Mudra

As per yoga the tip of the nose, the sense of smell, and the Muladhara Chakra are directly connected. This connection is well explained by the theory of acupressure. As per the concept of Chinese meridians the point 'GV 25' of the governing meridian is situated over the tip of the nose which gets stimulated as one concentrates here while practicing Nasikagra Drishti Mudra. This point is one of a very significant terminal points of governing meridian. This meridian is one of the two most important extraordinary meridians int he body, and it runs along the back median line.

This meridian emerges at the surface in the perinium area, runs to the tail bone, coccyx, and up the back of the body, over the head and ends on to the upper lip. Second extraordinary meridian, conception meridian begins at the perinium, point CO 1, runs ups along the frontal medial line and ends up at the upper lip as well. Both these meridians are thus connected in a yin-yang relationship, stimulation in one of them affects the flow of energy in the other.

As the point 'GV 25' located on the governor meridian is stimulated by the practice of Nasikagra Drishti Mudra it affects the flow of energy in the conception meridian too. As this stimulation in the conception meridian travels along its length and reaches the point 'CO 1' located at the perinium the Muladhara Chakra receives a activation push. Similarly, the Ajna and the Muladhara Chakras are also connected via the conception and the governor meridians.

Traditional functions of the point 'GV 25' located on the nose tip include the raising of the yang, restoring energy of and clearing the senses which leads to the increased power of concentration. This also increases the flow of energy towards the head which facilitates meditative states of mind. All the yang energies are created from the yin - the earth - and always flow upwards in the body. Point 'GV 25' raises the yang up along with also stimulating the conception meridian which is yin.

CHAPTER 10

Trataka on Thumb (Thumb – Gazing)

10.1 Trataka on Thumb

Gazing on the thumb's nail is one of the very effective ways of practicing Trataka. Rather since the thumb can be moved to various other points (left shoulder, right Shoulder, between the eyebrows, tip of the nose) considered good for gazing, it can be used for creating a sequence wherein one can gaze on all these points one after the other.

10.2 Technique of Thumb Gazing

- Sit in any comfortable meditative posture, keep the body relaxed and the spine erect.

- Hold the right hand directly at a two-hand spans distance in front of the nose, at nose level, the elbow slightly bent.

- Make a fist of this hand with the thumb positioned vertically upward.

- Fix the gaze on the tip of this thumb, try not to blink the eyes.

- Move the thumb and bring is to the tip of the nose, constantly gazing at the tip of the thumb.
- Stay here for a while, now move the thumb back to the starting position.
- Keeping the head steady, only the eyes will follow the tip of the thumb, start to slide the thumb towards the far end of the left shoulder keeping it at the nose level, go until one gets the double vision of the tip of this thumb, stay here for a while.
- Slide it back to the starting position, throughout maintaining the eye contact with the tip of the thumb.
- Now turn the thumb upside down (thumb of the other hand can also be employed here) and bring it to the centre of the eyebrows, Stay here for the same duration as earlier after which bring it back to the starting point in front of the nose.
- Release the hand and close the eyes for a while until they are completely relaxed.
- Slowly open the eyes.
- Likewise, repeat the same sequence with the left hand towards the right shoulder.

This is one round.

Breathing Pattern, Duration, and Repetitions

Practice two rounds of Trataka (Thumb gazing) in a single sitting, not more than twice a day. Inhale while moving the thumb towards the nose or the center of the eyebrows, and exhale while moving it towards either shoulder.

10.3 When to avoid doing Trataka (Contraindications)?

Persons suffering from the following conditions should not do Trataka:

- Retinal disease,
- Myopia,
- Cataract,
- Vertigo.

Avoid doing Trataka while wearing lenses or spectacles.

You may feel a burning sensation in your eyes and a natural tendency would be to drop your eyelids. One of the reasons for burning sensation could be strain in your eyes. Soften your gaze to eliminate the strain.

You might get a slight headache. That could happen due to the deliberate movement of the eyes which are not used to such movements. If you close your eyes for a few seconds, the headache should disappear.

10.4 Benefits of Thumb Gazing

- It improves the quality of concentration.
- All the six major muscles surrounding each eye get strengthened.
- Vision improves in both, individuals with any vision issues or no prior vision issues.
- It improves the peripheral vision to a great extent.

- The memory receives a boost.
- A large number of brain centres remain inactive, dormant for normal individuals, practicing Trataka activates them up.
- The thought process and reasoning ability get more clear and sorted.
- It improves memory.
- The consciousness of the Mind gets boosted.
- It is a path to deeper meditation.
- The practitioner attains peace of mind, stability and clarity of thoughts.

CHAPTER 11

Dakshinajatru and Vamajatru Trataka (Gazing on Right and Left Shoulders)

Gazing on the right shoulder is also known as Dakshinajatru Trataka (gazing on the end of the right collarbone). Similarly gazing on the left shoulder is also known as Vamajatru Trataka (gazing on the end of the left collarbone).

11.1 Dakshinajatru Trataka (Right-Shoulder Gaze)

- Take up a comfortable sitting posture such as the Sukhasana or Vajrasana.
- Make sure that your body is erect and that your head is steady and neck straight.
- Clench the fingers of your right hand with the thumb perpendicular to the fist as if performing the Shiva Linga Mudra.
- Lift and stretch the hand in front with your elbow straight so that the vertical right thumb is in front of you at eye level.

- Keep your left hand on your left thigh.
- Fix your gaze on the nail of the right thumb.
- Slowly and smoothly move your right hand in a wide arc towards your right shoulder while keeping your gaze fixed on the thumb nail.
- Move only the eyeballs and not your head as you follow the thumb to the tip of the right shoulder.
- Hold the position for 15 to 30 seconds and then slowly come back to the front position.
- Go as slowly and consciously as possible and hold the gaze without blinking.
- Relax your right hand back to the thigh.
- After completing the practice, gently close your eyes. Rub your palms against each other, form a cup of your palms and cover your eyes.
- Relax by feeling the warmth and darkness in your eyes for about 30 seconds.
- After sufficient relaxation, gently drop your hands down.
- Feel the cool sensation around the eyeballs. Relax for a few seconds. Do not open your eyes immediately.
- Repeat the practice thrice at each sitting.

11.2 Vamajatru Trataka (Left-Shoulder Gaze)

- Take up a comfortable sitting posture such as the Sukhasana or Vajrasana.

- Make sure that your body is erect and that your head is steady and neck straight.

- Clench the fingers of your left hand with the thumb perpendicular to the fist as if performing the Shiva Linga Mudra.

- Lift and stretch the hand in front with your elbow straight so that the vertical left thumb is in front of you at eye level.

- Keep your right hand on your right thigh.

- Fix your gaze on the nail of the left thumb.

- Slowly and smoothly move your left hand in a wide arc towards your left shoulder while keeping your gaze fixed on the thumb nail.

- Move only the eyeballs and not your head as you follow the thumb to the tip of the left shoulder.

- Hold the position for 15 to 30 seconds and then slowly come back to the front position.

- Go as slowly and consciously as possible and hold the gaze without blinking.

- Relax your left hand back to the thigh.

- After completing the practice, gently close your eyes.

- Rub your palms against each other, form a cup of your palms and cover your eyes. Relax by feeling the warmth and darkness in your eyes for about 30 seconds.

- After sufficient relaxation, gently drop your hands down.

- Feel the cool sensation around the eyeballs.

- Relax for a few seconds.

- Do not open your eyes immediately.

- Repeat the practice thrice at each sitting.

CHAPTER 12

Trataka on Self-Reflection in Mirror (Mirror–Gazing)

12.1 Trataka on Image of Self-Reflection in Mirror: (Mirror-Gazing)

To do mirror gazing, you use a mirror to make eye contact with your own reflection instead of closing your eyes and turning your attention inward. This practice can become deeply intimate, since it requires you to spend a few quiet, mindful moments sitting with not just your thoughts, but your own watchful eyes.

Perhaps you harbour mixed feelings toward yourself or your reflection and consider the mirror your own personal antagonist. If you avoid looking into mirrors to keep from triggering internal conflict or self-loathing, mirror gazing might prove a challenging exercise… at first. Over time, however, you may find it promotes a new, more positive perspective.

12.2 What makes Mirror Gazing different from other Forms of Trataka?

As a meditative practice, mirror gazing isn't different from other mindfulness exercises. It still helps you learn to stay more conscious of the present moment, and it still offers the chance to find a sense of relaxation and grounded calm amid the various stressors you face each day.

Two main differences set mirror gazing apart: the use of a mirror, and the focus on coming face-to-face with yourself to learn more about your inner thoughts and feelings.

How can looking at your own face improve self-awareness or strengthen the traits you value most?

12.2.1 Why is it effective?

If eyes, as people say, offer a window into your soul, mirror gazing provides a direct route to the heart of your distress, making it easier to explore emotional symptoms and identify underlying causes.

12.3 Some potential Benefits of Mirror-Gazing

- Greater self-compassion.

- Looking at yourself in a mirror might make you feel uncomfortable when your reflection reminds you of imperfections and weaknesses. But mirror gazing can help you embrace a more realistic, forgiving perspective. Sure, you have a few flaws, but who doesn't? These less-than-perfect characteristics don't make you any less worthy of love — your own love most of all.

People often avoid thinking about mistakes they've made or wish they could change aspects of themselves they consider flawed. But in the mirror, you can't turn away from errors and imperfections. One option remains: acknowledging them.

Reminding yourself that everyone makes mistakes can help you forgive your own errors and put a stop to hurtful self-criticism.

Similarly, the compassionate acknowledgment of your unique self can help disrupt feelings of shame or your own unworthiness. Pruning back negative thoughts that spring up like weeds can, in turn, allow self-acceptance and self-love to bloom.

12.4 Authenticity and Emotional Awareness

People accustomed to pushing down difficult emotions often grow used to hiding how they truly feel. Your mirror won't let you hide from anything, though. Unpleasant feelings, worries, and self-doubt all surface, breaking through the mask you put up in front of others.

Emotions commonly show up on your face, but research shows that you can carry pain elsewhere in the body, too. Distress might be evident in the slump of your shoulders, a restless foot, or your inability to meet your own gaze. Looking at yourself, though, makes it easier to practice authenticity. You can't get away from the things troubling you, so you have to confront them instead.

Noting the emotions shifting across your face and showing in your body language can help you take stock of your present state of mind, behind false fronts of cheer and calm. As you fully open yourself to what comes and relax into the experience instead of fighting it, you may even find that sitting with distress dulls the edges of the sharpest pains, making them easier to bear.

Learning to tolerate, or better yet, openly accept all emotions (even the uncomfortable ones) can also make it easier to communicate honestly with others.

12.4.1 Stronger Sense of Self

Spending more time with yourself allows you to know yourself better.

You're in the best position to affirm and validate all of your traits. When opinions and criticisms of others fray your self-worth, leaving you feeling vulnerable and alone, you can find a trusted friend simply by turning to your mirror. This knowledge can strengthen you, leaving you feeling whole instead of fragmented and making it easier to cope with unkind words and judgment.

12.5 How to do Mirror-Gazing?

If you typically don't spend much time in front of a mirror, looking into your own eyes might make you a little uncomfortable. Regardless of any awkwardness you might feel, commit to giving it a try for a week or two.

Reports from people who tried mirror gazing suggest that doing it for 10 minutes a day can help ease stress and increase self-compassion.

You'll need a mirror large enough to see your face. It's also best to use a mirror that stands on its own, since holding one up for 10 minutes may prove distracting (if not difficult).

- Find a quiet place and get comfortable in a chair or on the floor.

- Angle the mirror so you can easily make eye contact with your reflection.

- Set your timer. If 10 minutes feels too long, start with 5 minutes. There's no need to set a specific meditation goal. Your aim is to sit with yourself, as reflected in your mirror.

- Close your eyes and slow your breathing. Take several deep breaths, allowing yourself to inhale, hold, and then slowly exhale.

- As your body relaxes, let yourself breathe naturally. Turn your attention to any tense spots in your body and visualize that tension slowly dissolving with each breath.

- Open your eyes and look into the mirror. Pay attention to the rhythm of your breath. Does it feel or sound any different as you gaze into the mirror?

- Consider the message in your eyes. Is it critical or kind? Do you immediately focus on something specific you dislike about yourself? Visualize each slow breath dissolving that dislike.

- What thoughts come to mind? Does a little voice begin to name flaws, one after the other? Do you find it hard to hold your gaze because of any self-disdain?

- As each thought comes up, observe it and let it pass. Pay attention to the way your emotions move across your face. What does judgment look like? Anger? Fear? Acceptance?

- If you find yourself grasping at any feelings that come up, or narrowing your focus to a particularly critical thought, gently return your attention to your reflection. Let your thoughts travel where they will, but hold your gaze, looking at yourself with kindness, as they wander.

The bottom line

While mirrors may seem an ideal tool for prioritizing appearance and other physical traits, they can actually reveal much more. Gazing into a mirror makes it possible to face your emotions and the reactions that accompany them. It also helps you learn to counter self-judgment with appreciation, compassion, and love.

There's more to you than the way you look. As contrary as it may seem, your mirror often holds the key to the depths of your true self.

CHAPTER 13

Trataka on Nabhi (Manipura Chakra): Mirror-Gazing

13.1 Trataka on Nabhi (Manipura Chakra): Navel Gazing

Navel-gazing or omphaloskepsis is the contemplation of one's navel as an aid to meditation.

The word derives from the Ancient Greek words omphalos (navel) and sképsis (lit. viewing, examination, speculation).

Actual use of the practice as an aid to contemplation of basic principles of the cosmos and human nature is found in the practice of yoga or Hinduism and sometimes in the Eastern Orthodox Church. In yoga, the navel is the site of the manipura (also called nabhi) chakra, which yogis consider "a powerful chakra of the body". The monks of Mount Athos, Greece, were described as Omphalopsychians in the 1830s, who pretended or fancied that they experienced celestial joys when gazing on their umbilical region, in converse with the Deity.

However, phrases such as "contemplating one's navel" or "navel-gazing" are frequently used, usually in jocular fashion, to refer to self-absorbed pursuits.

Decoding Sutra 3.30: How Concentrating on the Navel Encourages Body Awareness, Patanjali's Yoga Sutra 3.30 says that:

nabhichakre kayavyoohajnanam

Meaning: On the navel circle (comes) the knowledge of the constitution of the body.

In this sutra, the power or practice Patanjali describes is "samyama on the navel." This concentrated meditation on your midsection opens the door to a vital understanding of your body's constituent parts and subtle-energy channels (nadis).

Vibhuti Pada (the chapter on manifestation) with its reference to samyama, which can be loosely translated as "integration." Patanjali writes that samyama is the simultaneous expression of the last three limbs of Ashtanga Yoga—dharana (concentration), dhyana (meditation), and samadhi (realization)—it's a total absorption into the object of meditation in order to experience profound shifts in awareness.

Some of the superhuman powers achieved through samyama, such as shrinking yourself into a minute size or becoming extra heavy, seemed the stuff of Marvel Comics. The samyamas are expressions of deep realizations that are part of a continuum of understanding.

13.1.1 The Power of Navel-Gazing

In this sutra, the power or practice Patanjali describes is "samyama on the navel." This concentrated meditation on your midsection opens the door to a vital understanding of your body's constituent parts and subtle-energy channels (nadis). Your manipura (navel) chakra is the originating point of 72,000 nadis, making it a particularly potent region.

This exalted practice even has a counterpart in ancient Greece, where navel-gazing, or omphaloskepsis (omphalo = navel; skepsis = inquiry), was considered an appropriate mode of philosophical pursuit. In fact, four Roman statues depicting men standing in a circle with their hands on their hips looking down at their bellies is preserved at the Louvre. The difference is that the Greek version is a symbolic, philosophical gazing, while the yogic version is a complete absorption into the subtle center itself.

Further, Yoga Sutra 1.12 says:

abhyasavairagyabhyan tannirodhah

Meaning: Their control is by practice and non-attachment.

The mind, to have this non-attachment, must be clear, good and rational. Why should we practice? Because each action is like the pulsations quivering over the surface of the lake. The vibration dies out, and what is left? The Samsharas, the impressions. When a large number of these impressions is left on the mind they coalesce, and become a habit. It is said "habit is second nature;" it is first nature also, and the whole nature of man; everything that we are, is the result of habit. That gives us consolation, because, if it is only habit, we can make and unmake it at any time. The Samshara is left by these vibrations passing out of our mind, each one of them leaving its result. Our character is the sum-total of these marks, and according as some particular wave prevails one takes that tone.

The commanding energy exists in the presence of navel centre with this practice. You can start by simply staring at your bellybutton and then closing your eyes, continuing to visualize it. As you centre-on the site of your former umbilical cord, you'll begin to experience a type of listening that frees your mind from overthinking and allows the grace of samyama to begin. This may result in your point of focus shifting deeper toward your spine on its own accord and opening your awareness to a new field of energy.

If you find the concept of samyama on the navel confusing, you can get a taste of samyama in other ways. Just observe how asana and pranayama can sometimes seem to stop time. Your thoughts become more spacious and you can catch a glimpse of the almost ungraspable now (presence)—the goal of a yoga practice. You may also become acutely aware of the musculoskeletal aspect of each asana as you stretch, release, and strengthen. You may understand, for the first time, how your feet connect to and affect your spine—or how postures affect breathing, which in turn affects your mind—and vice versa. These are the types of realizations that precede samyama.

While the suggestion of "perfect knowledge of the disposition of the human body" may elude us, we can gain insight into our own bodies and minds by attending to the physical, mental, and energetic aspects of yoga. All experiences and understandings are coloured by what you bring to them, and thus it is likely that you'll have a different journey with this sutra.

Whether seated or practicing asana, pay attention to your navel without forcing an outcome. Listen. Do it again. Stay open to new experiences. Take your time. Let the beauty of Vibhuti Pada unfold.

The term "navel gazing" is used to refer to intense self-reflection, often with the implication that the individual doing the gazing is self-absorbed or that he or she is too focused on a single issue, at the cost of ignoring other important issues. Being accused of navel gazing isn't necessarily a bad thing; sometimes a little bit of contemplation can be a productive pursuit, especially when someone is trying to reach a decision about something important.

13.2 Navel-Gazing in different Traditions

References to navel gazing appear to have emerged from observation of certain religious ascetics; observers believed that some religious practitioners were staring at their navels to enter deep meditative reveries. It is certainly true that some meditation poses place people in a prime position for this process, and contemplating one's own navel could have powerful connotations in religions where people view the navel as the center of life or as an energy source.

Many cultures, including the Greeks, associate tremendous power with the navel. Obviously, the navel is a connection to the life-force of one's mother, through the umbilical cord, so in some cultures, it is viewed as a centre or starting point. In several societies, people have specified particular sites as the "Navel of the World," ranging from Delphi to Easter Island. These sites were believed to have religious significance as centres of culture and religion for members of these societies.

Navel gazing is also used in terms of describing an act of intense introspection; an act where one is taken over by intense feelings and thoughts about one's life. The thoughts and emotions are usually deep and leave the person contemplating about his life, the decisions that he has taken, and where he has gone wrong (it could include several other types of thoughts as well). Even though the person is rather preoccupied with his own thoughts, this form of navel gazing is not tinged with a degrading connotation. It is, on the other hand, taken as a positive sign where a person involved in the act reaches an important decision after much introspection.

Hinduism believes that navel gazing, as a part of yoga, is a very fruitful form of meditation. Staring at one's navel, blocks out all distractions, thus allowing one to focus on his breathing without the clamoring of unnecessary thoughts, and thereby reaching a state of calmness. The navel is also considered a powerful chakra (Manipura chakra) of energy in yoga teachings.

Many cultures of the world associate the navel with something that is tremendously powerful. In fact, it is usually given the position of being the centre of energy, the very starting of life. The umbilical cord that connects an unborn child with its mother finds its way through the navel. And therefore, the very start of life has the navel at its centre. The importance, significance, and symbolism placed with the navel thereof is undeniable.

If used in the right way, navel gazing can be a powerful medium that allows the practitioner to peep inside the mind of the character and understand him better. However, it needs to be used tastefully and with a lot of discretion. If overused, it can lose its purpose and become just another (annoying) tool.

CHAPTER 14

Bindu Trataka
(Gazing at a Point or Dot)

14.1 Bindu Trataka (Gazing at a Point or Dot)

In the beginning of trataka meditation we must start with dot-gazing trataka, just as you cannot go to second standard without being successful in first class, similarly bindu trataka plays an important role in all trataka meditation. This solves the problem of our eyes. And if any problem in the eyes like watery or blurred vision goes away.

This practice is the initial practice of all Trataka, because only with this we are able to progress to the next stage, in other words, we enter the state of Trataka. Bindu Trataka should be practiced in a quiet and clean room where there is pure air of vitality.

14.2 What is Bindu-Trataka Meditation?

Often the question of people remains that how can one get good experiences in short time in Trataka? Such people want to take the mental and spiritual benefits associated with Trataka in the shortest possible time. In such a situation, if we do such a practice in the beginning which will make you worthy of practicing Tratak. The only purpose behind getting Bindu trataka meditation done first is that.

- It avoids some side effect of Trataka.
- It take less time to experience great results.
- It helps us to take advantage of personal, psychic and spiritual growth.

14.3 How to Practice Bindu-Trataka Meditation?

Before starting practice of trāṭaka, the practitioner should ensure that there is no disease in his eyes. If there is any type of disease in his eyes, he should not follow practice in such a state. First of all, he should get treatment from a doctor, then he should start practice only after the disease is completely cured. If the practitioner has any kind of disease in his eyes and even then he does practice, his disease can be spread further and there is also a fear of getting the eyes defective. Trāṭaka should be practiced only with healthy eyes.

An āsana (meditative mat) should be made before practice. The āsana should be an insulator of energy. It can be made up of Kush (a thin grass). A blanket may also be used as āsana. After making a thin fold of the blanket, a pure white cloth should be spread over it. The Asana can be made up with a thin sheet of sponge. A white cloth should be spread over it. It should always be kept in mind that the Asana should not be too soft nor should it be so harsh that it gets the feet pricked.

- First put a chart on the wall. Put cello tape on the corner of the chart. Put such cello tape on the corner to form the chart stick. The chart has got to be kept very straight. There shouldn't be any shrinkage within the chart. It should be absolutely flat.

- Now take a sketch pen. Draw little Circle ('Bindu' or 'Point'). The tiny circle (point or 'Bindu') is to be drawn with the sketch pen on the chart at such an area in order that there's no problem in 'Bindu trataka meditation'.

- The point should be exactly parallel to the eyes. Keep some extent with maximum diameter of two mm. In 'Bindu trataka meditation', why make dots smaller? The sight that comes from the eyes within the sort of Teas comes out like rays of sunshine within the sort of light and therefore the rays are opened up, so once we attempt to collect the rays at some point and, therefore, the smaller the object, f the rays emanating from the eyes are concentrated during a small space, then those rays become equally powerful.

- The practitioner who wants to try to 'Bindu trataka meditation' must be one meter aside from the chart.

- Now do your posture at a distance of 1 m.

- Now sit on the pedestal (Posture).

- Sitting on the asana, calm the mind and remain still, after that comfortably focus your eyes on the point. When the mind is calm then we see the point comfortably and correctly.

- Care is usually taken that on the posture, we sit in 'Sahaj asana Mudra'.

- The spine should be straight.

- Take some soft cloth. When you do Bindu trataka meditation, there's also itching within the eyes, burning sensation, and tears. So we don't need to scratch our eyes during this situation. But wipe it lightly with a soft cloth.

- Keep in mind that your distance should be one meter from point.

- The point on the chart should be placed at an area which is at the level of your eyes.

- You have only got to ascertain this dot. Don't consider anything while doing Trataka and don't look here and there. Just consider the dot (Bindu). Sukshma can mean 'small' or 'subtle.' In the practice of trataka an object is gazed at until its subtle form manifests in front of the closed eyes.

- And know one thing, the place where you're practicing the trot point shouldn't be very windy, that is, choose such an area where there's no wind on your eyes.

- Due to this, if the wind blow are going to be considerably on the eyes, then there'll be some problems within the eyes and therefore the eyes will blink.

- The fan shouldn't be run within the room where you're practicing Trataka. There's no atmospheric pressure within the eyes.

- Look at the object (dot) carefully without blinking your eyelids.

- For as long as you'll see, the Bindu) has got to be seen in 'Bindu trataka meditation'.

- Do not stare at the point. Look at it normally with your eyes. Initially, watch it only for 10 seconds because it causes dryness in the eyes and they start making you uncomfortable.

- If you gaze forcefully, it can make you uncomfortable with practice. So watch it comfortably.

- After a few days of practice, you are able to see normally for a longer time. When the practice increases, then we feel that a wave of light is coming out of the eyes and is encircling the point.

- Gradually it becomes brighter. And when we practice, the point starts appearing bright not black.

- This colour shows that your confidence is increasing and you can focus more and more with practice.

- After this, when more days are passed, wherever we look with a calm mind, a wave of light is felt coming out of the eyes.

14.4 Interesting Facts about Bindu-Trataka Meditation

It is the beginning of all trataka practice, this is because only by this we can easily enter other states. If we want to understand in simple words, then we are able to establish that harmony in our mind and brain which is necessary in Tratak. Without this, if we do other exercises, then the chances of success remain 90%.

This is just because we are not prepared for beginning and small steps, entering the high-level stage will not be able to harmonize our body and mind. If you also want to awaken your subconscious mind with Trataka, never directly do other exercises like Shakti chakra Trataka, mirror Trataka, candle gazing Trataka. Your brain can become entangled in those experiences.

14.5 Benefits of Bindu Trataka

- Practicing Bindu trataka meditation improves the eyesight. The weakness of the eyes is removed. The eyes get used to the practice of Trataka.
- The mind becomes calm.
- We connect with ourselves more and more.
- Improved memory and increased IQ.
- Better control over thoughts and feelings.
- An unprecedented increase in self-worth.
- Enhanced sense of general well-being.
- A more open and friendly attitude generally.

CHAPTER 15

Trataka on Aum (Om) Symbol

15.1 Primordial, Perennial, Universal (Aum) 'Om': Introduction

The first and the most important word in the post-Vedic, Vishwamitra-Gayatri is **'OM'** (or AUM). Om is a sacred syllable representing Brahman, the impersonal Absolute, omnipotent, omnipresent, the source of all manifest existence. Brahman, in itself, is incomprehensible; so a symbol is used to help us realise the Unknowable. Om is said to be the essence of all mantras, the highest of all mantras, the Divine Word or Shabda Brahman. It gives power to all mantras. Hence all mantras begin with Om and without it are said to be deprived of power. Om is the sound of the infinite. Om is said to be 'Adi Anadi', without beginning or the end and embracing all that exists. Om moves the *prana* or the cosmic vital force. Hence it is called *Pranava*.

The importance of Om is evident from the fact that Saint Dnyaneshwar, a renowned Indian saint who lived in state of Maharashtra during the period 1275–1296, begins his Dnyaneshwari, a vernacular commentary on the Bhagavad Gita by addressing *Parmatman* as *Om* and paying obeisance to Om. He says therein that the Vedas describe Om and conversely also implies that the Vedas have emerged from Om.

In the linguistic sense, Om is a word from the Sanskrit language having its own root. It is derived from the root "*ava*" which is in the sense of *raksanam*: protection, and also sustenance. Therefore, "ava - man" means the one who protects and sustains this entire creation (*jagat*) by lending his existence and consciousness. By the rules of Sanskrit grammar, the suffix "man" in the word "ava - man" loses the last vowel and what follows it, which gives "avam". Through vocalization process, "va" becomes "u". Further "a" and "u" combine to form the diphtong "aum", finally yielding Om.

Phonetic significance of Om: Every form of this creation (universe) is the God's form and the name for that form is the God's name. If the God is all and you want to give the God a name, a name not in any particular language or alphabet, a name that is purely phonetic, that includes all the names that are there, what should you do? In any language, when a person opens the mouth and makes a sound without any other effort, it is "a". When you close the mouth and make a sound it is "m". All other sounds in any language fall between "a" and" m". All the words in all languages are made up of letters, and the letters are, even if there is no script, are sounds. The one sound that represents all these sounds produced by the letters "a - u - m ", is OM. It is the sound, which does not require the need of your tongue; so even a person who cannot speak (a dumb, for example) can produce this great sound of OM, without any effort.

"Om it idaṃ sarvam" (Taittirīya Upaniṣhad 1.8) "This whole world is OM". The syllable OM, also known as Aum and Pranava, is the most sacred symbol of Hinduism, Buddhism, Jainism, Sikhism and Zoroastrianism. It is used both as a symbol and as a sound in religious worship, ritual chanting, performance of sacraments and rituals, meditation and tantra. In Hinduism it is venerated as Brāhman ('Brahma Nada' or 'Pranava Nada') in the form of syllable (Akshara) and sound (Shabda). Om is believed by many as "Apaurusheya" (not of human origin).

Initially, in the early Vedic period, because of the sanctity associated with it, the word was kept as a secret and never uttered in public. It was used in private conversations and passed on from the teacher to the disciple or father to the son directly and in secrecy. It was also not used in the rituals. Because it was not permitted to use the word directly, some early Upanishads referred to it indirectly as the udgita (upsound) or pranava (calling out), alluding to its significance in regulated breathing and religious chanting respectively.

15.2 'Om' is Primordial

OM or AUM is not just a sound a vibration. It is not just a symbol. It is all that is within our perception and all that is beyond our perception. It is core of our existence. OM was revered before the birth of all the religions in the world. The origin of "Big-Bang" is from the experiments made by Dr. Robert Wilson and Dr. Arno Penjias on microwave radiation in the universe. During their studies they were continually getting some unknown radiation from the universe. This radiation associated with the body at a temperature of 3 degrees Kelvin and it is presumed that the radiation must have emanated when Big-Bang took place. Actually their experiment proved the reverberation of the Big-Bang explosion with which the universe began. Synonymous to this, our scriptures state that the sound OM or AUM – the Pranava mantra – was the first energy created at the time of disturbance of the equilibrium. It has been accepted in Hindu Religion that AUM – the first **primordial** sound energy ('Brahma Nad') emerged in the process of creation. Hence, what the scientific experiments revealed as microwave reverberations during the Big-Bang is already explicitly explained by our scriptures in the form of 'AUM'. "Om is the primordial throb of the universe. It is the sound form of Atma (Consciousness)." – Maitri Upanishad. According to Guru Granth Sahib, the most sacred book of Sikhs, The name of the Creator (OM or Ik Onkar) is True In The Primal Beginning; True Throughout The Ages. (1–4, Japu, Mahalla 1)

15.3 'Om' is Apaurusheya

OM is the soundless sound of existence, which the Zen Buddhists refer to as 'the sound of one-hand clapping'. The sound of 'OM' is known as 'Anahata', which means un-struck sound. All other ordinary sounds in the universe emerge as a result of frictional force between any two or more objects. Therefore the 'OM' sound cannot be generated by person. It is self-producing sound. It is Apaurusheya. OM stands outside of history: as the distillation of the wisdom of the Vedas, the syllable remains "beyond human origin" (*apauruṣheya*), eternal, prior to everything (Pūrva Mīmāṃsā Sūtra 1.1.27–32).

15.4 'Om' is Perennial

OM is the akshara, which literally means immutable or imperishable, or perennial: the characteristic of the Syllable 'OM' as mentioned in the scriptures subsequent to Rig

Veda. Therefore OM is perennial, meaning that, it timeless, everlasting, which is valid in the past, present and future. As mentioned earlier, even Guru Granth Sahib mentions this to be perennial.

15.5 'Om' is Universal

OM is not related to any particular religion. As stated earlier, 'OM' is revered in many religions in the world: Hinduism, Buddhism, Jainism, Sikhism, and Zoroastrianism, to name a few. It is therefore 'Universal'.

15.6 'Om' in Ancient Texts

Before we refer to the mention of OM in the ancient Hindu texts, including Vedas, Upanishads, Smriti texts, Puranas, Bhagavad Gita etc, let us first briefly introduce these Hindu texts.

There are two historic classifications of Hindu texts: **Shruti** – that which is heard, and **Smriti** – that which is remembered.

The *Shruti* refers to the body of most authoritative, ancient religious texts, believed to be eternal knowledge authored neither by human nor divine agent but transmitted by sages (*rishi*). These comprise the central canon of Hinduism. It includes the **four Vedas** including its four types of embedded texts - **the Samhitas, the Brahmanas, the Aranyakas** and the early **Upanishads**. Of the *Shrutis* (Vedic corpus), the Upanishads alone are widely influential among Hindus, considered scriptures par excellence of Hinduism, and their central ideas have continued to influence its thoughts and traditions.

The **Smriti** texts are a specific body of Hindu texts attributed to an author, as a derivative work they are considered less authoritative than *Sruti* in Hinduism. The Smriti literature is a vast corpus of diverse texts, and includes but is not limited to Vedāngas, the Hindu epics, the Sutras and Shastras, the texts of Hindu philosophies, the Puranas, the Kāvya or poetical literature, the *Bhasyas*, and numerous *Nibandhas* (digests) covering politics, ethics, culture, arts and society.

15.7 'Om' in Hinduism

15.7.1 OM in Rig Veda

Although the oldest scripture in Hinduism is known to be 'Rig Veda' (the first of the four Vedas), ironically it does not mention about 'OM' directly; rather it indirectly refers to it as 'Akshara' (Rig Veda, 1.164.39).

Richo akshare parame vyoman, yasmin deva
adhi vishve nishedhuhu|
Yasthannaveda kim richa karishyathi, yayithath
vidu stha ime samasathe||

Meaning: Richa is situated in akshara. knowledge is structured in consciousness, the non-changing transcendental basis of all relative existence in which reside the impulses of creative intelligence responsible for the whole manifest universe. He whose awareness is not open to this level of reality, what can these eternal expressions of knowledge accomplish for him?

OR, in other words:

"He who knows not the eternal Syllable (Akshara) of the Veda, the highest point upon which all the gods repose, what business has he with the Veda? Only its knowers sit here in peace and concord".

The akshara literally means immutable or imperishable, or perennial: the characteristic of the Syllable 'OM' as mentioned in the scriptures subsequent to Rig Veda.

15.7.2 OM in Yajur Veda

Yajurveda Chapter 40 is also called Isha Upanishad. It says:

> Om krato smara. Vayur-anilam-amrtam athedam
> Bhasmantagm sariram,
> Om krato smara krtagm smara, krato
> smara krtam smara. (40.17)

Meaning: O men, at the time of death remember OM, the name of God. Think about God and yourself, think about the deeds you performed in your entire life. The vayu takes the soul. And remember that the body is mortal and will be finally destroyed.

> O3m krato smara |

'O3m' is the highest reality. Here, the number intervening between o and m refers to 3 aspects of 'om' – (1) the sound originating in muladhara, (2) proceeding toward chest and (3) entering and spreading in the head; it spreads in three vyahruti- bhu, bhuvah, svah. Therefore 'OM' is also referred to as 'AUM', where 'A' represents Agni, 'U' represents Vayu, and 'M' represents Aditya.

15.7.3 OM in Aitareya-Brahmana

> Om ityasau yo'sau [sûryah] tapati.
> – Aitareya-Brâhmana (5.32)

Meaning: That which glows [i.e., the Sun] is Om."

15.7.4 OM in Brihadaranyaka Upanishad

yō ha vai jyēṣṭhaṅ ca śrēṣṭhaṅ ca vēda
jyēṣṭhaśca ha vai śrēṣṭhaśca
bhavati prāṇō vāva jyēṣṭhaśca śrēṣṭhaśca || 5.1.1 ||

Meaning: Om is Brahman, the Primeval Being. This is the Veda which the knowers of Brahman know; through it one knows what is to be known".

15.7.5 OM in Chandogya Upanishad

ōmityētadakṣaramudgīthamupāsīta.
ōmiti hyudgāyati tasyōpavyākhyānam (1.1.1)

Meaning: One should meditate on this syllable: Om. That is the quintessence of the essences, the Supreme, the highest.

Sa esha rasana rasatamah paramah
paradhyorashtamo yadudgeethah. (1.1.3)

Meaning: The syllable OM which is called Udgitha, is the quintessence (means the most perfect) of the essences, the supreme, deserving of the highest place.

This can be said, because Om is the Primal Word, the Original Sound, the First Word "spoken" by God, and by which all that "is" was created, and is being sustained and evolved at this very moment.

Tadetanmithunamomityetasminnaksharesagvung
srijyate yada vai mithunau
samagachchata aapayato vai tavanyonyasya kamam. (1.1.6)

Meaning: Speech and breath are joined together in the Syllable OM.

Omiyetadaksharamudgeethamupasitomiti hyudgayati tasyopavyakhyanam. (1.4.1)

Meaning: One should meditate on Om.... This sound is that syllable, the immortal, the fearless. having entered this, the gods become immortal, fearless. He, who knowing it thus, praises this syllable, take refuge in that syllable, in the immortal, fearless sound, and having entered it, he becomes immortal, even as the gods became immortal.

Athadhyatmam ya evayam mukhyah pranastmudgeethamupasitomiti hyesha svaranneti(1.5.3)

Meaning: The breath is continually sounding Om.

Sa esha parovariyanudgeethah sa eshonnatah parovariyo hasya bhavati parovariyaso ha likajjayati ya etadevam vidvanaparovariya samugeethamupaste. (1.9.2)

Meaning: This is the Udgitha (the song as OM, which uplifts the singer), the most excellent; this is endless. He who, knowing this, meditates on the Udgitha; obtsins progressively the most excellent life and wins the most outstanding worlds.

Tanyabhyatapattebhyobhitaptebhya omkarah samprasravattadyatha shadakuna sarvani paranani. Santrinnanyevamomkaren sarva vakasantrinnomkara eveda sarvamomkara eveda sarvam. (2.23.3)

Meaning: As all leaves are held together by a stalk, so is all speech held together by Om. Verily, the Syllable Om is all this- yea, the Syllable Om is all this.

Tadyatha aahapath aatata ubhau gramau gachchateemam chamum chaivamevaita aadityasya rashmay ubhau lokau gachchanteem chamum. Chamushmadadityatpratayante ta aasu nadishu sripta aabhyo nadibhyah pratayante teyamushminnadte sriptah. (8.6.2)

Meaning: Even as a great extending highway runs between two villages, this one and that yonder, even so the rays of the sun go to both these worlds, this one and that yonder. They start from the yonder sun and enter into the. They start from the naadis and enter into the yonder sun.… When a man departs from this body, then he goes upwards by these very rays or he goes up with the thought 'Om.' As his mind is failing, he goes to the sun. That, verily, is the gateway of the world, an entering in for the knowers, a shutting out for the non-knowers.

15.7.6 OM in Katha Upanishad

Sarve Veda Yatpadmamananti tapasi sarvani cha yadvadanti. Yadichchanto brahmacharyam charanti tatte pada sangrahen braveemyomityetat. (15)

Etaddhyevaksharam brahma etaddhyevaksharam param. Etaddhyevaksharam gyatwa yo yadichchati tasya tat. (16)

Etadalambanam shreshthametadalamanam param. Etadalambanam gyatwa brahmaloke maheeyate. (17)

Meaning: That word which all the Vedas declare, which all the austerities proclaim, desiring which people practice brahmacharya, that word, to you I shall tell in brief: It is Om.

This syllable is, verily, the everlasting Spirit. This syllable is, indeed is the highest end; knowing this very syllable, whatever anyone desires will be his. This support is the best. This support is the highest; knowing this support, one becomes great in the world of Brahma.

15.7.7 OM in Mandukya Upanishad

Om ityetadakshamida sarvam tasyopavyakhyanam.
Butam bhasva bhavishaditi sarvamomkar aiv.
Yachchanyat trikalateetam tadapyomkar aiv. (1)

Soayamatmadhyaksharamomkaro adhimitram pada
matrashcha pada
Akar ukaro makaar iti. (8)

Amatrashchturtho vyavahatyah pranchopeshamah shivo advait.
Evamomkar aatmaiva samvishatyatmanam ya evam veda. (12)

Meaning: Om: this syllable is all this.... All that is the past, the present and the future, all this is only the syllable Om. And whatever else there is beyond the threefold time, that too is only the Syllable Om.... The Self is of the nature of the Syllable Om.... Thus the Syllable Om is the very Self. He who knows it thus enters the [Supreme] Self with his [individual] Self.

Om-ity-etad-aksharam-idam sarvam, tasyopavyakhyanam
bhutam bhavad bhavishyaditi sarvam-omkara eva.
Yaccanyat trikalatitam tadapy omkara eva.

– Mandukya Upanishad 1. 8. 12

Meaning: All is OM: Hari Om. The whole universe is the syllable Om. Following is the exposition of Om. Everything that was, is, or will be is, in truth Om. All else which transcends time, space, and causation is also Om.

> *Soayamaymadhyakshamonkaroadhimatram pada matra matrashcha akaar ukaro makaar iti.*
> *Dhanur gṛhīvtā aupaniṣadam mahāstram śaram hy upāsā-niśitam samdadhīta, āyamya tad-bhāvagatena cetasā lakṣyam tad evākṣaram, saumya viddhi (2.2.3).*

Meaning: Taking as the bow the great weapon of the Upanishads [Om], one should place in it the arrow sharpened by meditation. Drawing it with a mind engaged in the contemplation of That [Brahman], O beloved, know that Imperishable Brahman as the target.

15.7.8 OM in Prashna Upanishad

> *Etadvai satyakaam param chaparam cha brahma yadonkarah.*
> *Tasmadwidwanetenaivayatanainaikataramanveti. (5.2.2)*

> *Yah punaretam trimatrenomityetenaivaksharen param purushamabhi dyayaeet sa tejasi surye sampannah. Yatha padodarastvacha vinirbhuchyat evam ha vai sa papmana vinibhuktah sa samabhirunneeyate brahmalokam sa etasmajjeevaghanat paratparam prushatam purushameekshate. Tadetau shlokau bhavatah. (5.2.5)*

> *Rigbhiretam yajurbhirantariksham samabhiryata tat kavayo vedayante. Tamonkarenaivayatanenanveti vidvan yattachchantamajaramamritamabhayam param cheti.*

> *– (5.2.7)*

Meaning: Satyakama, son of Shibi, asked [the Rishi Pippalada]: 'Venerable Sir, what world does he who meditates on the Omkara until the end of his life, win by That?' To him, he said: 'That which is the Omkara, O Satyakama, is verily the higher and the lower Brahman. Therefore, with this support alone does the wise man reach the one or the other.'... If he meditates on the Supreme Being [Parampurusha] with the Syllable Om, he becomes one with the light, the Sun. He is led to the world of Brahman. He sees the Person that dwells in the body, who is higher than the highest life.... That the wise one attains, even by the Omkara as a support, that which is tranquil, unaging, immortal, fearless, and supreme.

15.7.9 OM in Shvetashvatara Upanishad

Udgeetametatparam tu brahma tasmimstrayam supratishthaksharam cha.
Atrantaram brhmavido viditva leena brahmani tatpara yonimuktah.
(Shvetashvatara Upanishad 1:7)

Meaning: Om has been sung as the supreme Brahman, and in it are the Triad [the individual spirit, the cosmos, and the Cosmic Spirit]. It is the firm support, the imperishable. The knowers of Brahman by knowing what is therein become merged in Brahman, intent thereon and freed from birth.

Vahneryatha yonigstasya murtinar drishyate naiva cha linganashah.
Sa bhooya evendhanayonigrihya stadvobhayam vai pranaven dehe. (1.13)
Svadehamaranim kritva pranavam chottararanim.
Dhyananirmathanabhasadevam pashyannigoodhavat. (1.14)

Meaning: As the form of fire when latent in its source is not seen and yet its seed is not destroyed, but may be seized again and again in its source by means of the drill [a pointed stick whirled to produce fire for the Vedic sacrifices], so it is in both cases. The Self has to be seized in the body by the Pranava. By making one's body the lower friction stick and the Pranava the upper friction stick, by practicing the friction of meditation one may see the hidden God.

15.7.10 OM in Bhagavad Gita

Raso aham aapsu kauntuya prabhutva sasi suryaha pranava vedasu sabda hai paurasam nrasu.

(7:8)

Meaning: O son of Kuntī, I am the taste of water, the light of the sun and the moon, the syllable Pranava (OM) in the Vedic mantras; I am the sound in ether and ability in man.

Omityekaksharam Brahma vyaharanmamanusmaran.
Yah prayati tyajandeham sa yati paramaam gatim. (8:13)

Meaning: Uttering Om, the single-syllabled Brahman, meditating on me, departing thus from his body, he attains the Goal Supreme.

Pitahamasya jagato mata dhata pitamahah.
Vedyam pavitramonkar riksaam yajureva cha. (9.17)

Meaning: I am the father of this Universe, the mother, the support, and the grandsire. I am the object of knowledge, the purifier and the syllable om. I am also the Rig, the Sama, and the Yajur [Vedas].

Maharishinaam Bhriguraham Giramasmyekamaksharam.
Yagyanaam japayagyosmi sthavarannam himalayah. (10.25)

Meaning: Of the great sages I am Bhrigu; of vibrations I am the transcendental om. Of sacrifices I am the chanting of the holy names [japa], and of immovable things I am the Himalayas.

Tasmaad Om iti udrahit yagya-dana-tapa-kriyaha.
Pravartak vidonokat satatma Brahma-vaadinam. (17:24)

Meaning: Thus the transcendentalists undertake sacrifices, charities, and penances, beginning always with OM, to attain the Supreme.

15.7.11 OM in Manu Smriti

The Laws of Manu (Manu Smriti) is the oldest code of laws in India.

Ekaksharam param Brahma pranayamah param tapah.
Saavitryastu param nasty maunatsatyam vishishyate.
– Manu Smriti, 2.83

Meaqning: The monosyllable Om is the highest Brahman. ... Undoubtedly a Brahmin reaches the highest goal by japa of Om alone, whether he performs other rites or neglects them.

15.7.12 OM in Mandukya Karika

Omkaram padasho vidyatpada matra na sanshayah.
Omkaram padasho gyatva na kinchidapi chintayet.
– Mandukya Karika, (1.24)

Meaning: Om should be known. Having known Om, one should not think of anything whatsoever.

> *Yunjeet pranave cheetah pranavo brahma nirbhayam.*
> *Pranave nityktasya na bhayam vidyate kvachit. (1.25)*

Meaning: One should concentrate one's mind on Om, for Om is Brahman beyond fear. For a man, ever fixed in Brahman, there can be no fear anywhere.

> *Pranavo hyaparam brahma pranavashcha parah smritah.*
> *Apoorvo anantaro bahyo naparah pranavo vyayah. (1.26)*

> *Sarvasya pranavo hyadiramadhyamantastathaiva cha.*
> *Evam hi pranavam gyatva vyashnate tadanantram. (1.27)*

> *Pranavam heeshram vidyatsarvasya hridi sansthitam.*
> *Sarvavyapinamonkaram matva dhhero na shochati. (1.28)*

> *Amaatro anantamatrashcha dwaitasyopashamah shivah.*
> *Onkaro vidito yena sa munirnataro janah. (1.29)*

Meaning: Om is surely the lower Brahman; and Om is considered to be the higher Brahman. Om is without cause, and without inside and outside; and it is undecaying. Om is indeed the beginning, middle, and end–everything. Having known this way indeed one attains immediately identity with the Self. One should know Om to be God seated in the hearts of all. Meditating on the all-pervasive Om, the intelligent man grieves no more. The Om, without measures and possessed of infinite dimension, is the auspicious entity where all duality ceases. He by whom Om is known, is the real sage, and not so is any other man.

15.8 Four States of Aum (Om)

According to the science of mantra, there are four kinds of sound waves- standing waves, reverberant waves, oscillating waves, and transcendental waves. The mantra 'OM' produces all of these waves. Om is a combination of three sounds 'A', 'U' and 'M'. 'A' creates the standing wave, 'U' the reverberant wave, and 'M' the oscillating wave. The fourth wave, being transcendental and beyond the sense of hearing or speech, is created by meditating on Om in the heart centre. When we transcend the external sensory world, we become aware of high frequency waves which have no rest period. Ordinary waves have a rest period. When we chant the mantra 'OM', it begins and it ends. The beginning and the end are the rest periods for the sound wave. But when we transcend the mind, then we come to a high sound frequency which has no rest period. The first three sound waves belong to the three dimensions of human consciousness and are interconnected. 'A' represents the waking or sense consciousness, 'U' the dream or sub-consciousness, and 'M' deep sleep or unconsciousness. The fourth wave represents the unlimited dimension of consciousness which is beyond the mind and the senses. Therefore, we can say that Om has four bases: the sensual world, the mental world, the terrestrial world, and the ultimate state.

The sacred OM is the primordial sound from which the whole creation has manifested. It is compared to the so called scientific big bang theory. The Mandukya Upanishad deals with this topic in detail. The sound Om is divided in four stages or parts. A.U.M. and the silence afterwards. These four represent the four states of human life, viz., the waking, dream, deep sleep and *turiya*. They also represent the three bodies, viz., Gross body, subtle body and causal body and the turiya or transcendental reality. *Turiya* is not a name but an indication for the self which is the subtlest state or the transcendental meditation state in which the body is completely at rest but the mind is fully alert (a state of 'restful alertness'). OM (AUM) is the mystic name for the Hindu Trimurti, and represents the union of the three gods: "A" for Brahma, "U" for Vishnu and "M" for Mahadev, which is another name of Shiva.

Various states of consciousness are illustrated in the following from the symbol of OM:

Those Four are the Same with "A-U-M" and Silence: That Om, though described as having four states, is indivisible; it is pure Consciousness itself. That Consciousness is Om. The three sounds A-U-M (ah, ou, mm) and the three letters A, U, M are identical with the three states of waking, dreaming, and sleeping, and these three states are identical with the three sounds and letters. The fourth state, Turiya is to be realized only in the silence behind or beyond the other three.

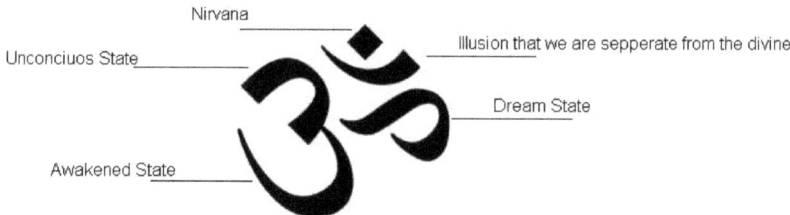

Decoding the symbol as written in Sanskrit brings deeper insight: the parts that resemble a "3" and an "o" represent three stages of the human mind's states of consciousness or progression from ignorance to clarity and the "cup shaped half circle" symbolizes that which separates these states from the "dot" which represents the true self.

Vaishvanara: the lower left curve (the bottom half of the "3") is waking state, the Conscious mind, which is focused outward to material objects and the gross or relative world.

Taijasa: (represented by the "o" to the right of the center of the "3") is the Dreaming state, active unconscious or the subtle world; that which is focused inward to only the thoughts in the mind.

Prajna: (represented by the top curve or upper part of the "3") is the Casual plane of existence, the dreamless deep sleep state, deep meditation and latent unconsciousness.

Turiya: (represented as a dot or point above the top curve") the Bindu, absolute, pure unity consciousness, Atman/Brahman/Self. The "True Self" in its most un-worldly and purest consciousness (where) *"awareness of the world and of multiplicity is completely obliterated* «. Turiya, "the true self", is separated from the other 3 states by a horizontal curve, the Nadi which means Sound; this is how Maya, the illusory world, the manifest or relative is transcended.

15.9 Bindu Trataka on the Symbol of AUM

Any sadhaka desiring to do Trataka on the symbol of AUM should focus on the Turiya or Nirvana (represented as a dot or point above the top curve in the figure of AUM.

The steps for Bindu Trataka are the same as have already been spelt out in the previous chapter.

At present, many people practice trāṭaka on the image of 'Om'. There are various types of portraits found in the market on which Om is written. The practitioners buy and bring portraits of Om of their choice and practise on it. Now-a-days, a plenty of special types of portraits of Om are found in the market. In the middle of the portrait, a small Om is written and circular lines are formed around it. These lines are formed in such a way; it seems that the Om is at very far away place. If you will gaze these circular lines, it will appear that these lines are bustling. Such a scene is formed in our brain, as if there is some motion in these circular lines. The truth is that there is no movement of any kind in these lines, these movements are happening in our brain. Vibrations actually occur in the vrittis in the form of tejas emerging from our eyes, but it appears that there is a movement in the circular lines.

Those practitioners who do not want to practise trāṭaka at the dot or on the photo, they should practice trāṭak on Om. Many of the practitioners like to practise trāṭaka on the portrait of Om, it is good for them to practise on it. The practice of trāṭaka on Om should exactly be same as that of trāṭaka on dot, the method of practice of these two is the same.

But there is a different kind of feeling while doing practice of trāṭaka on Om than that of dot trāṭaka. The reason for that are the circular lines made around the Om. These lines have different effects on the brain while doing practice. These lines are seen spinning in a particular direction and a special kind of activity is felt in the brain. But when the restlessness of the mind will gradually subside (during the practice of trāṭaka), then there will be no feeling of any kind of bustling on the brain and the circular lines made around Om will also appear to be stabilized at their place. When it happens, it should be understood that the mind of the practitioner has started to become stable.

While doing practise on Om, the colours of those five elements will appear sequentially. It depends on the practice of the seeker that after how many days, these five elements will appear and after how much practise the elements will change colours. When the practice will be of months, the same blue rays will be visible. Continue your practise in the same state. After having much practice, the Om can be visible in the state of meditation or in the state of dreams.

The practitioner has to decide while starting the practice of trāṭaka on which object should he begin practise. At the initial stage, there are three options — (i). Practice of trāṭaka on dot (ii). Practice of trāṭak on portrait of god, (iii). Practice of trāṭaka on the portrait of Om etc. Out of these three, practice of trāṭaka should be done on any one. It is not necessary to practise on all of these, because the results of practising trāṭaka on all of these are the identical.

The important point is the purpose for which the practice of trāṭaka is being done. If he is practising only to bridle the fickleness of mind, then he should continue his practise in the same manner. If the practitioner is a seeker and is also practising yoga or he has the objective of doing some tasks in the future by trāṭaka, he should try to proceed further i.e. he should proceed towards the next stage of trāṭaka. Such practitioners even though they have visualized the colour of the Ākāśha Tattva, their mind has begun to be calm and introverted, but do not do the mistake to think that you have become a good practitioner. The truth is that you have just started the practice of trāṭaka, this path goes a very long way. It is such a science that when you will enter it, you have to take it for a number of years to go deeper in it and to understand it minutely and also to become versatile in this study by rigorous practise and at last, your present age will be left short, but still practice of trāṭaka will be left.

CHAPTER 16

Trataka on Sri Yantra

16.1 Trataka: Meditation on the Form of Sri Yantra

The mind can be steadied by practicing repeated concentration and meditation on a visual form. The particular form can differ according to the individual's temperament and taste. Some examples are: the steady flame of a candle, a picture of a beloved saint or teacher, the symbol OM, a yantra, etc. Form meditation usually begins with trataka or steady gazing at the physical picture of the form. As you practice this, you may simultaneously repeat your chosen mantra. This steady gazing progresses into clear mental visualization of the object of concentration. An example of form meditation is given below:

Trataka is a very simple and common exercise used to train the mind to remain absolutely still and without thoughts.

On a white paper take a print of the Shri yantra. (preferably a line diagram) This is the energy geometry of your own self, use this always for any mediation etc where you need a focus point. While choosing an image to print, remember that the central triangle is perfectly equilateral and the central dot/Bindu is in its exact centre. Mark the central dot with a pen to make it clearly visible (If you use this image below, shade in the central dot completely and dark black.)

A yantra is a mystic symbol in the form of a geometric diagram. Those who went into deep meditation experienced something in the unconscious levels of the mind. Upon returning to normal consciousness, they expressed what they had experienced in the form of mantras, or mystic sounds, and yantras.

This yantra is a diagram of the cosmos. The dot in the centre represents the absolute consciousness. The surrounding circles are the subtle expressions of the three forces of nature which begin to manifest as the yantra spreads outward.

16.2 How to do Trataka Meditation with Shri Yantra?

Decide where you will sit, be comfortable. Paste this paper on the wall a few feet away from your seat at the eye level. Now steadily gaze at the central dot/Bindu without blinking your eyes, till your eyes start tearing up. When it becomes too much, close your eyes, you will see the after image of the dot and the geometry in your closed eyes. Then again open your eyes and stare at the dot without blinking. Repeat this exercise till you can stare for longer and longer duration. The after-image in your closed eyes will become stronger and stronger and eventually the entire Yantra will remain imprinted in your closed eyes as an after image. (If you can sit in on your asana in a yogic posture like Siddhasana or Padmasana it will be faster, if you cannot for some reason, that also is ok.)

Here you are training your internal geometry also. You are showing your energy how it looks in its perfectly balanced state. You should do this steady gazing/Trataka as much as you can, start for one minute a day and gradually increase it. Soon your personal energy will start entraining itself with the Shri yantra geometry and resonating with it. Later you will also see how the 2-D paper geometry changes, becomes deeper adding more depth and dimensions to it. It is a wonderful experience!

When you do Dhyana (meditation) and search for the gold/silver – flame/point of the third eye chakra within yourself, the forces of aakshepa and vikshepa interfere and push/pull your focus away from that specific point. (Aakshepa means the energy which tosses aside, throws away with force, presents a challenge i.e. the tossing mind. Vikshepa is the wandering mind, it means to scatter, to repel (exactly like same pole magnets), to disperse.)

If you have practiced doing Trataka on the Shri yantra, these forces will be overcome faster and you will be able to access the opening of the Brahmanadi faster.

1. Position the yantra so its centre is at eye level and a comfortable distance away. Sit with your spine straight. Breathe in and out slowly until your breath flows naturally.

   Begin with your eyes open, simply gazing at the yantra. Look at the centre or 'dot' which represents the unity that underlies all the diversity of the physical world. The key is to maintain a receptive, alert frame of mind, without drawing any conclusions, and free of concepts or thoughts. As you feel yourself gathering consciousness, allow yourself to flow with the momentum of this consciousness.

2. Now allow your eyes to see the triangle that encloses the dot (Bindu). The downward-pointing triangle represents the feminine creative power, while the upward facing triangle represents male energy.

3. Allow your vision to expand to include the circles outside of the triangles. They represent the cycles of

cosmic rhythms. The image of the circle embodies the notion that time has no beginning and no end.

4. Bring your awareness to lotus petals outside the circle. Notice that they are pointing outwards, as if opening. They illustrate the unfolding of our understanding.

5. The square at the outside of the yantra represents the material world that our senses show us and the illusion of separateness via the well-defined edges and boundaries. At the periphery of the figure are four T-shaped portals, or gateways. Notice that they point toward the interior of the yantra, the inner spaces of life. They represent our earthly passage from the external and material to the internal and sacred.

6. When your awareness begins to shift inward, close your eyes. Now watch the yantra imprinted in your mind's eye, allowing it to gradually guide you within.

7. Do nothing, and you will find yourself participating in pure consciousness without the mind defining it.

8. The patterns of creativity represented by these primordial shapes express the fundamental forces of nature. They govern the world and they govern you. When you are ready, you may wish to take a deep breath, begin to move your toes and fingers, open your eyes, and become aware of your surroundings once again.

Maha Meru Mantra

"Om Shreem Hreem Shreem Kamle Kamalalaye Praseed, Praseed, Shreem Hreem Shreem Om Mahalaxmaye Namah"

16.3 Benefits of Trataka Meditation with Shri Yantra

- Yantras add value to one's life and do have mystical powers to heal certain issues which are not understood by most of the people.

- Increases the intensity of prayers and makes the thoughts more strong and influential.

- When you focus at the centre of Yantra, a time will come when mental chattering starts to descend and focus starts to ascend, resulting in a one-pointed focus.

- Increase your self-awareness & illuminates a clear path to your inner self.

- It empowers your inner self with the clarity to understand and explore the change in the outside.

- It helps in the opening of your 7 chakras.

- Attainment of wisdom that will rocket you towards your desires.

- Turns you into an unstoppable magnet for attracting those people and wisdom into your reality.

- Open the knots of past karmas, external setbacks that are holding you back from your destiny.

- It brings good fortune, wealth and prosperity to one's life.

The regular practice of Sri Yantra meditation calms one's mind and brings mental stability, which certainly helps in making the right decisions of your life be it in a business job or relationship.

CHAPTER 17

Trataka on Image of Guru or Deity (Murti-Trataka)

17.1 Trataka on Guru Murti

Through Antar trataka meditation, we practice getting into our inner selves. Different trataka meditation practices have different effects on us, so you can choose them based on your understanding. Murti Trataka Meditation is practiced by first focusing oneself on some medium and when it reaches the eyes, then it is done by doing trataka in its inner.

17.1.1 Guru Murti Trataka Meditation or Sadhana

The only difference between different types of trataka is the medium on which we do the practice. If this practice is done by connecting it with faith, we have the possibility of having a spiritual experience. Guru Murti Trataka Sadhana is one of those phases of Trataka in which we develop psychic powers and abilities.

The Trataka should not be practiced alone. If you want to get success in Trataka, then you have to first practice how to control body and mind. If you are not able to do this then you can only get physical experience in the Trataka meditation practice. You have to travel a long way in psychic and spiritual experience. Therefore, first of all, do trust meditation and see if you are ready for trataka gazing meditation practice.

Any image or medium means to restrain one's ideal and worship. The simple meaning of restraint is to create the quality of any medium in oneself. Here, in practice we can take Guru Murti or Dev Murti as the medium but do not forget to do worship and Prana Pratishthan before practice. All you have to do is sit in front of the idol in the simple sitting position and do trataka gazing meditation. This exercise is in 3 stages, like;

17.2 Step-by-step Guide of How to Perform Guru-Murti Trataka Meditation

Before practicing Guru Murti Trataka, you should test yourself whether you can do better Trataka on Aradhya Dev (Deity) or Guru. Most people do trataka without a guru, in such a situation, if they do trataka by considering Lord Ganesha as their adoration, the success is achieved in awakening the Third eye chakra.

The purpose of Guru Murti trataka meditation is also to awaken the pineal gland. Our faith and rituals also increase with this trataka. At the same time, we become stronger at the mental level. Some people believe that this practice is very helpful in starting and maintaining psychic powers.

(i) Trataka with open eyes

Sit in front of the idol and after worshiping, take all the attention to your eyes. You must have already learned to focus yourself on any part of the body by the meditation method. After this, you have to do trataka meditation on the eyes of the idol for some time.

(ii) Psyche meditation with closed eyes

In this step, you have to close your eyes and perform trataka on the same idol with closed eyes. You can also call it mindfulness meditation. Its purpose is to travel only inside you. Second, when your concentration starts increasing, you become able to remain stable for a long time.

(iii) Journey of the inner world

When you do trataka with closed eyes, you learn to control yourself and when this happens you start the journey of the inner world with closed eyes. During the inner journey, the process of purification of your mind begins. Performing trataka on the deity and Manas Puja further helps in dividing this body made up of five elements.

- Take a 2-inch-long and 3-inch-wide photograph of your favored deity or your favourite Holy Person, Saint, or Sadguru. You can practice on statues or images or photographs as their result remain the same.

- Fix this statue or image on the wall at 3.5 feet height, so you can sit comfortably and practice on it.

- Now sit down on a Yoga mat or Asana at a distance of 3.5 feet from a wall or you can take distance as long as your straight hand. Distance depends upon how comfortable you can practice.

- Do some yogic exercise that makes your eyesight relax and then practice on this guru Murti or any other image placed on the wall. Practice shouldn't be more than 20–25 seconds or as long as you can open your eyes.

- Now immediately close your eyes and bring that image to your Third eyes. This is your forehead place.

- Practice this for some time and reach up to 10 attempts of practice. Then try to close your eyes and visualize this murti on your third eye and stay on this.

- Stay in this state as far as you can. You get an amazing result if you stay in this trance state for a long time.

Guru Murti trataka meditation is the best spiritual practice for Sadhaka (devotee). You experience psychic ability development as well as some spiritual benefit also.

17.2.1 What is the meaning of the Guru Statue?

The purpose of the adorable deity idol is to achieve success in Trataka by using your feelings and morale. While doing trataka on the idol, you automatically feel an inclination in your thoughts. Therefore it can also be said that Guru Murti Trataka Sadhana also works to strengthen our faith and rituals.

Whenever you go to the temple, your mind starts becoming pure after getting rid of the unwanted intrusive thoughts and negative feelings inside you. In such a situation, Guru Murti Trataka meditation plays an important role in feeling and maintaining that state for a long time.

17.2.2 Use of mantras during trataka meditation

Although there is no need to chant any mantra in Guru Murti Trataka, but to bind the mind, you can chant Guru Mantra or Beej Mantra of Aradhya Dev.

17.3 Miracles of Guru-Murti Trataka Meditation

Not only Guru Murti, but all other Trataka meditations are associated with some experience or the other. Therefore, if we talk about this trataka, we can get to see spiritual experiences and miracles in it, such as third eye chakra activation, knowledge of time, and Sadguru's guidance. According to some experience, through this practice, they have seen his adoration directly.

17.4 Story of Eklavya as Guru's Statue Trataka Practice

Since ages, the story of Eklavya (a character from the Indian epic- Mahabharata) has come to define exemplary discipleship. But there is an unheard and unseen side to the famous story.

Eklavya was the son of a poor hunter. He wanted to learn archery to save the deer in the forest that were being hunted by the leopards. So he went to Dronacharya (a master of advanced military arts) and requested him to teach him archery. Dronacharya was the teacher of the Royal family.

In those days, as a rule, a teacher to the members of Royal family was not allowed to teach the state art to anybody else. It was forbidden to make anyone as powerful as the princes for the safety of the region.

But Eklavya deeply desired to study under Dronacharya. Dronacharya, bound by the state law, could not accept him as his student.

Eklavya in his heart had already accepted Dronacharya as his Guru. He went home and made a statue of his Guru. Over the following years, with sincerity and practice, he learnt archery and became better than the state princes at the art. He became so good at it that, he would hear the sound of the animal, shoot an arrow at it and claim the animal.

One day, Arjuna, the prince found out about this talented archer. Making matters worse, he saw that Eklavya was far better than him. He went to Eklavya and asked him, 'Who taught you archery?'

'Dronacharya,' said Eklavya.

Hearing this, Arjuna was furious. He went up to Dronacharya and said angrily, 'What is this? You have cheated us. What you have done is a crime. You were supposed to teach me exclusively, but you taught this man and made him more skillful than me.'

Dronacharya was baffled and confused at Arjuna's allegations. He wondered who this student of his was, who had learned the art from him but whose name and identity he did not know! He thought hard but could not come up with an answer for Arjuna. He could not believe that this student was better than even Arjuna.

Both, Dronacharya and Arjuna decided to meet the boy.

Eklavya welcomed his master with great honour and love. He led both of them to the statue he had made of Dronacharya. Eklavya had practiced archery over all the years, considering and believing the statue to be his Guru.

In ancient times, a common practice in learning was- Guru Dakshina, where a student would give a token of gift or fee for the knowledge gained by the student.

Dronacharya said, 'Eklavya, you must give me some Guru Dakshina. You must give me the thumb of your right hand.' Eklavya knew that without the thumb, archery could not be practiced.

Eklavya without a second thought gave the thumb of his right hand to his Guru.

In this story Dronacharya is commonly viewed as being cruel and self-centred. The perceived understanding is, this boy who had learned the skill on his own and was good at it, is made to give it up for the vested interest of Dronacharya. But when one looked at it from the point of view of the wise, one finds, if it were not for this incident, nobody would have ever known Eklavya.

Though on the outside, it seemed as if Dronacharya had done injustice to Eklavya, actually Dronacharya uplifted Eklavya from just being a student to becoming an epitome of discipleship.

Dronacharya blessed Eklavya with immortality by asking him for his thumb. So when people think of devotion, they think of Eklavya, and not Arjuna.

See the greatness of Dronacharya, he took the blame on him and uplifted his student. That is why, even if the Guru is wrong, if your devotion is there you can never go wrong. But the Guru is not wrong, it appears he was partial but he uplifted Eklavya and preserved his Dharma (duty) also.

17.5 Trataka on Deity (Ishta Devata)

Keep the picture of your Ishta Devata (Deity) in front of you. For example, how to do Trataka on Lord Vishnu.

> "Dhyeya sada savitri mandala madhyavarti,
> Narayana sarasijasana sannivishta;
> Keyuravan, Makara kundalavan, kirti harih hiranmaya vapuh;
> Dhrita sankha chakra gada pane dvarakanilayachyuta."

Meaning: Fix the mind first on the feet of Lord Vishnu, then on lotus under the legs. Take it round the yellow silken cloth the Pitambara, then to the golden Hara, the gem on the breast, then ear-ring, then the face, then the crown on the head, then the bracelets on the arm, then the disc in the right upper hand, then the conch in the left upper hand, then the Gada or mace in the left lower hand. This is the order. Then come down to the feet and start again to the upper parts. Do like this again and again.

Whenever the mind runs away, fix it again and again, just as Lord Krishna says in the Gita VI-25:

> "Yato yato nischarati manaschanchalamasthiram
> Tatastato niyamyaitadatmanyeva vasam nayet."

Meaning: The conch represents 'OM' or Sabdha Brahman. The disk is the destroyer of the evil Vrittis or Vasanas, the mace represents the emblem of sovereignty, the lotus at the feet represents the world or universe.

At the outset, you can do Trataka, after taking Asana, on a find black point on the wall in front for 10 minutes. Slowly increase the time. Have a steady uninterrupted gaze on the dot without closing the eyes. You can also do Trataka after closing the two ears with your two thumbs, on the Anahat sound that rises from the Akasa of the heart. This will lead to actual Laya, in the long run. Then you can do Trataka on Lord Vishnu, Siva, Krishna or any other Murthy. Trataka practice gives tremendous power and removes a host of opthalmic ailments (eye troubles) and bestows Divya Drishti.

Those practitioners who are the followers of devotional path may practice trāṭaka on their tutelary deity, if they wish to do so. Such practitioners do not need to practice by making a dot on the chart paper. When you will practice on the image of a deity, the effect of different types of colours present on that image is there. It appears a little bit strange in the beginning, then it becomes a habit. Many practitioners practice trāṭaka on the portrait of their Ishta (chosen deity), they like it. But some practitioners feel uncomfortable in practicing on the portrait of their Ishta.

The seekers who wish to practice trāṭaka on the portrait of god should do the following:

- Buy a portrait of your favourite god, in whichever gesture you like, from the market and paste it on the wall, where trāṭaka has to be practiced.

- The method of pasting should be similar to that of chart paper; you may get the photo framed if desired. Make a small dot in the middle of eyebrows of the deity on that photo and practice trāṭaka on that dot. Practice of trāṭaka should be followed exactly as explained for a dot on a chart paper (Bindu Trataka).

- Do not mark a dot on the photo of the Deity. In such a situation, follow the practice of trāṭaka on the Bhrikuti (middle of both eyebrows) only.

- When it is required to close the eyes due to irritation in the eyes, then close your eyes.

- Keep the eyes closed for some time and do not try to open them.

- Then wipe the tears of the eyes slowly with soft thickened folded cloth which you have kept aside.

- At that time the eyes may have a burning sensation, let it happen. Do not put pressure on the eyes with fingers and even do not itch the eyes. In such a situation the seeker may definitely feel some discomfort or trouble. The seeker should tolerate this discomfort.

- When the practitioner is sitting with his eyes closed, he should try to mentally visualize the face of god. In the beginning, the portrait may not be seen with the closed eyes. After practicing as such for a few days, the mental image of the deity will begin to be formed. After the burning sensation of the eyes has receded, the practice of trāṭaka should be resumed.

CHAPTER 18

Research on Trataka and its Benefits

18.1 Trataka in Ayurveda for Curing Sleep Disorders

Today stress is major factor for initiating diseases and one of the commonest is Excessive Daytime Sleepiness (EDS). The causes and signs and symptoms of Tandra (sleep disorders) are similar to that of EDS; so it can be correlated with EDS. According to modern concept, Tandra can be correlated with Excessive Daytime Sleep (EDS), EDS is defined as "A state of impaired awareness associated with a desire or inclination to sleep". In modern science the treatment of EDS is done by drugs which are mostly depressants or sedatives. Though there are many researches carried on EDS, there is no proper line of treatment and it is an unsolved mystery of medicine.

Shatakarma is the part of yoga, trataka is one among shatkarma, it is indicated in tandra vyadhi (sleep disorders) as per Hatayoga pradapika. Trataka is a yogic kriya which has the ease of access, consumes less time and is cost effective.

Trataka or yogic routine with regards to concentrated gazing is an antiquated hatha yoga practice utilized for all round advancement of our body, brain and soul. The significance of word trataka is "to gaze steadily" or "to gaze distinctly". The idea of trataka is characterized unmistakably by a few yogis and old yoga writings like Hatha Yoga Pradipika:

Being quiet, a professional should look consistently at a little stamp (a little thing), till eyes are loaded with tears. This is called trataka by the âchâryas. (Hatha Yoga Pradipika, 2.31)

It goes under one of the shatkarmas or shatkriyas: six sanitization systems in hatha yoga intended to make the body solid and sound. It is a greatly intense strategy which encourages us to cure and enhance all eye issue, expels lethargy and controlling our mind. It really helps in coordinating the sensory system a distinct way and furthermore builds our vitality level. It quietens all our intellectual capacities and aides in accomplishing complete focus and true serenity.

18.1.1 Ayurveda's View on Tandra Vyadhi (Sleep Disorders)

Sushruta stated that 'duhkha' (grief) is the root cause of diseases-

> taddhukhasamyoga vyadhaya ucyante

Meaning: If one avoids duhkha, there would be no disease. In order to avoid, the removal of causes that are attributed with duhkha, needs attention.

Charaka has listed the causes for duhkha.

> Dhīdhrtismrtivibhramsha samprapti
> kalakarmanam| asatmyarthagamashceti
> jnatavya dukhahetava ||

Meaning: Derangement of intellect, restraint and memory, advent of time and action and contact with unsuitable sense objects should know as the cause of misery.

Charaka samhita has discussed three main reasons for disease:

> *...asatmyendriyarthasamyoga, prajnaparadha, parinamashceti trayastrividhakalpa hetavo vikaranam samayogayuktastu prakrtihetavo bhavanti"*

i. **Asatmyndriyarthasamyoga-** Is extreme use, under use and abuse of sense organs while aligning with their objects. That means indulging cognitive organs, viz., eyes, nose, ear, tongue and skin, in contrary methods cause disease. For instance, listening music in high decibels triggers ear related diseases, which is called 'aindriyaka'

ii. **Prajnaparadha-** Is intellectual blasphemy. Improper understanding of objects by intellect will result in adverse actions such as, negative thinking, misbehavior with noble people, lack of knowledge controlling mind, lack of good conduct are some of the reasons for intellectual errors.

iii. **Kala-** Is seasonal variation. Improper intake of food such as untimely consumption of eateries while ignoring seasonal changes etc., are due to kalaviparinama. Improper intake of food also causes lot of life style disorders such as stress etc. As an effect, people also suffer with stress/anxiety disorders, work tensions and so on and so forth.

18.1.2 Sushruta

Sushruta was an ancient Indian surgeon (who was possibly born in 7th century BC) and is the author of the book Sushruta Samhita, in which he describes over 120 surgical instruments, 300 surgical procedures and classifies human surgery in 8 categories. In the Sushruta School, the first person to expound Ayurvedic knowledge was Dhanvantari who then taught it to Divodasa who, in turn, taught it to Sushruta, Aupadhenava, Aurabhra, Paushakalīvata, Gopurarakshita, and Bhoja. He is credited with performing cosmetic surgery and especially with using forehead skin to reconstruct noses which were amputated as a punishment for crimes in his era. In ancient India Medical Science supposedly made many advances. Specifically these advances were in the areas of plastic surgery, extraction of cataracts, and dental surgery. There is documentary evidence to prove the existence of these practices.

In spite of the absence of anesthesia, complex operations were performed, the practice of surgery has been recorded in India around 800 B.C. This need not come as a surprise because surgery (Shastrakarma) is one of the eight branches of Ayurveda the ancient Indian system of medicine. The oldest treatise dealing with surgery is the Shushruta-Samahita (Shushruta's compendium). Shusruta who lived in Kasi was one of the many Indian medical practitioners who included Atraya and Charaka. Shushruta was one of the first to study the human anatomy. In the Shusruta-Samahita he has described in detail the study of anatomy with the aid of a dead body.

18.1.3 Chestagaurav

The Modern name of Chestagaurav is Dyspraxia; Dyspraxia isn't a sign of muscle weakness or of low intelligence. It's a brain-based condition that makes it hard to plan and coordinate physical movement. Children with dyspraxia tend to struggle with balance and posture. They may appear clumsy or "out of sync" with their environment. Dyspraxia goes by many names: developmental coordination disorder, motor learning difficulty, motor planning difficulty and apraxia of speech. It can affect the development of gross motor skills like walking or jumping. It can also affect fine motor skills. These include things like the hand movements needed to write clearly and the mouth and tongue movements needed to pronounce words correctly.

18.1.4 Trataka as a Cure for Sleep Disorders

One of the Trataka techniques (like candle gazing) was successfully applied by some researchers on patients who were suffering from sleep disorders. The results were encouraging.

18.2 Effect of Trataka on Pulse Rate of College-Level Male Students

A research study shown changes the pulse rate by acute effect of Trataka practice. The purpose of the study was to compare the pulse rate between pre-test and post-test of college levels male students. For this study total 06 college-level male students were purposively selected from the Visva-Bharati University, Santiniketan, Bolpur, West Bengal, India. Their age ranges were from 18–22 years. For this study the measured pulse rate, with the help of experts who helped to conduct the test. Before recording the parameter, the subject was asked to relax physically and mentally for few minutes. Pulse rate was recorded by Fully Automatic Blood Pressure Monitor Device. Using at the Brachial Artery, the pulse rate was taken from device screen. For the collection of data pulse rates in pre- and post-test were taken. The selected subject underwent an acute effect of Trataka training and they carried out Trataka program for 15 minutes at evening sessions, under the instruction and supervision of the supervisor and others experts. In all cases, 't' test was applied, significant at 0.05 level of confidence. There were significant differences on pulse rate (MD = 5.66, SDD = 4.41 and SEMD = 1.80) ['t'= 3.144 > 2.571, has been found after acute effect of Trataka practice. The pulse rate was significantly reduced after Trataka practice.

18.3 Effect of Trataka on Critical Flicker Fusion (CFF) and Cognitive Performance

A study was conducted to evaluate the immediate effect of trataka on critical flicker fusion (CFF). CFF is defined as the frequency at which a flickering stimulus is perceived to be continuous. Thirty healthy volunteers were assessed in two sessions, i.e., a trataka and a control session. There was a significant increase in CFF following trataka, suggesting changes at the cortical level in the processes that mediates fusion.

Another present study was designed to assess the immediate effect of trataka on cognitive performance using the Stroop color-word test. A self-controlled study design was used. Each participant was assessed during two sessions (a trataka and a control session) on two separate days. Half of the participants practiced trataka on the 1st day and the control session was carried out on 2nd day. The remaining participants reversed the order of the sessions. Participants were alternately allocated to either schedule to prevent the order of the sessions influencing the outcome. The duration of both sessions was 25 minutes. Participants were assessed before and immediately after each session.

The participants were given 15 days of training in trataka. Pre-recorded audio instructions for trataka were played during the session. Trataka practice consisted of two distinct stages. The first stage consisted of eye exercises, which was a preparatory practice for trataka. The eye exercises included eyeball movements in horizontal, vertical, and diagonal directions and circular movements. These were performed with the eyes open, in a well-lit room. This was followed by the practice of palming to relax the eyes. Palming consists of putting slightly cupped palms over the eyes, so that the eyes perceive complete darkness. The first stage lasted for 10 minutes.

The second stage was trataka, and it was practiced in a dark room. The participants were asked to fix their gaze on the flame of a candle for approximately 2–3 minutes, suppressing the urge to blink as far as possible. Then they were asked to visualize the candle flame in between the eyebrows. This process was repeated for two to three rounds. Finally, the participants were asked to defocus, and the practice ended with silence and prayer. The second stage lasted for 15 minutes. The duration of the whole practice was 25 minutes.

During the control session, the participants practiced eye exercises for 10 minutes, and then for the next 15 minutes, they sat quietly with their eyes closed without doing any concentration or trataka.

Trataka showed better performance on the Stroop color-word test compared to the control session, suggesting increased selective attention, cognitive flexibility, and response inhibition following trataka.

18.4 Effect of trataka on the Visual Perception of Elderly People

Visual perception is the ability to interpret the surrounding environment by gathering information that is contained in visible light. The resulting perception is also known as eyesight, sight, or vision (visual, optical, or ocular). Visual perception is constructive in nature; that is a coherent whole is generated from ambiguous fragments that are encountered in dynamic visual scenes. Creating this coherent whole from fragmented sensory inputs requires one to detect, identify, distinguish and organize sensory input.

The purpose of this research was study is to find the effect of Trataka Kriya session on Visual Perception of Elderly people. Thirty Elderly People were taken as the subjects for the study. The age of the subjects ranged from above 60 years. The design used for the study was pre-post design. Stratified sampling technique was used for the subject's selection.

The study was performed on the Visual Perception of Elderly People; pre- and post- data for the study were assessed on the scoring and norms of the tests conducted. It included OMKAR Chanting, Trataka Kriya and Relaxation done by closing eyes until the inflammation feeling in eyes ends were used as the components of the session for a period of 6 Weeks. Dependent t-test was used for comparing the means of pre- and post-data between both the groups. Results: Though there was not significant level of change in level of Visual Perception, yet there was a little improvement observed in case of Visual Perception after the end of session for 6 weeks.

The results conclude that the Session for a longer duration may have highly significant level of change in the level of Visual Perception of Elderly People.

18.5 Effect of Prandharana and Trataka on Orientation Ability of Physical Education Students

The objective of this study was to find out the significant difference between adjusted post-test means of experimental groups (Prandharana and Tratak) and control group in relation to Orientation Ability. Ninety male physical education students from Madhya Pradesh were selected as subjects for this study. The age of the subjects ranged between 18–25 years. The subjects were divided into three groups i.e. two experimental groups (Prandharana and Trataka) mand one control group. For the study pre-test and post-test randomized group design, which consisted of one control group (n=30) and two experimental groups (n=30 in each) was used. Equal numbers of subjects were assigned randomly to the groups. Two groups (Prandharana group and Trataka group) served as experimental groups on which treatment was assigned and the third group served as the control group. Pranadharana means to be aware of your own breath. The experimental groups were imparted thirty minutes of daily practice of pranadharana and trataka, respectively, for ten weeks under the proper supervision and guidance of the scholar while no practice was imparted to control group. In order to find out the effect of Prandharana and Trataka on Orientation Ability, Analysis of Co-Variance (ANCOVA) was used. The level of significance was set at 0.05 level.

Significant difference was found among the adjusted post-test means of experimental groups and control group in Orientation Ability, since the F-value (15.058) was found significant at .05 level with 2, 86 df. Trataka Group proved to be superior than Pranadharna Group in Orientation Ability.

18.6 A Comparative Clinical Study to evaluate the efficacy of Jyoti Trataka and Eye exercises in the management of Prathama Patalagata Timira w.s.r. to simple Myopia

Eye is a highly specialized sense organ serving the most important function of vision. Vision is the most vital of all the senses. Almost 80% of knowledge is perceived only through eyes. Humans are mostly dependent upon the vision for their day-to-day work. Hence any hindrance to this means a major handicap. Ayurveda advises that all sincere efforts should be made to protect the eyes as long as one is alive. Ayurvedic classical texts have mentioned about eye and its diseases since Vedic and Samhita kala, thus showing the importance of eye and ways to protect it. In Ayurveda, clinical features related to visual disturbances are generally seen in Dristigata roga. The anatomical consideration of the Patala and symptoms of the vitiated Dosa situated in these Patala reveals that the word Timira which is described as an ocular pathology in Ayurveda, is nothing but error of refraction. The part of clinical features of Timira (Prathama Patalagata Timira) can be correlated to myopia.

Myopia or short sightedness is one of the errors of refraction characterized by poor/ blurring of distant vision. Simple myopia, the most common form of myopia, described as physiological error, develops in childhood and almost always increases in severity until middle to late teenage years. Later, it is usually not progressive or has low progression rate. Individuals with small degree of myopia may present with asthenopic symptoms. Myopia can be corrected optically by concave spherical lens or surgically by refractive surgeries such as LASIK (Laser in – situ keratomileusis).

As about 90% of visually impaired belong to developing countries, correction of refractive errors can be a financial burden. Yoga Shastra states that regular practice of trataka can cure eye diseases. It is a simple and cost effective non-pharmacological method. Eye exercises are also such simple, cost-effective non- pharmacological method being practiced in many parts of India for betterment of eyesight.

Objective of the present research study was to assess the effect of Jyoti Trataka in Prathama Patalagata Timira w.s.r to Simple Myopia.

For the current study, 40 subjects with simple myopia were selected and randomly grouped into two groups with 20 subjects in each group. Group-1 was advised with Jyoti Trataka and Group-2 with Eye Exercises for a period of 30 days. Follow up was done after 30 days of completion of the study. Assessment was done based on objective and subjective parameters.

Both the groups showed improvement in objective and subjective parameters within the groups. Jyoti Trataka group showed better improvement in objective and subjective parameters between the groups. Jyoti trataka group showed statistically highly significant results in objective parameters like clinical refraction (right and left eye), visual acuity (left eye and both eyes), and better results in visual acuity right eye. Significant results were found in subjective parameters like heaviness of eyes and better improvement seen in headache, eye strain, watering of eyes and pain in the eyes.

In the current study, Jyoti Trataka group showed better results in improvement of clinical refraction, visual acuity and asthenopic symptoms. Thus, this study may be concluded as regular practice of Jyoti Trataka is more effective in the management of prathama patalagata timira w.s.r to simple myopia.

18.7 Changes in Heart Rate Variability Following Trataka

Research studies have shown a shift toward the vagal tone during meditation. (Note; Vagal tone is activity of the vagus nerve, the 10th cranial nerve and a fundamental component of the parasympathetic branch of the autonomic nervous system. This branch of the nervous system is not under conscious control and is largely responsible for the regulation of several body compartments at rest). However, autonomic changes in trataka were not studied. The present study was planned to assess the changes in heart rate variability (HRV) following trataka. HRV and breath rate were assessed in thirty healthy male volunteers with ages ranging from 20 to 33 years (group mean age ± SD, 23.8 ± 3.5) before and after yogic visual concentration (trataka) and control session on 2 separate days. Repeated measures analysis of variance (ANOVA) were performed with two "within subjects" factors, i.e., Factor-1-Sessions; trataka and control and Factor -2-States; "Pre", and "Post". This was followed by post-analyses with Bonferroni adjustment comparing "Post" with "Pre" values. There was a significant decrease in LF (RM ANOVA with Bonferroni adjustment $P < 0.01$) and increase in high frequency ($P < 0.01$) after trataka. Breath rate ($P < 0.001$) and heart rate ($P < 0.01$) were significantly reduced after trataka as compared to before trataka. Control session showed no change. Thus, the practice of trataka leads to increased vagal tone and reduced sympathetic arousal. Though trataka is known as cleansing technique, it could induce calm state of mind which is similar to a mental state reached by the practice of meditation.

18.8 Unfolding Chakras by Trataka

How are chakras unfolded through trāṭak, what is its process?‖ First of all, you should understand about chakras. There are seven primary chakras in the human body. The names of these Chakras are as follows— 1. Mūlādhāra Chakra (Root Plexus), 2. Svādhiṣṭhāna Chakra (Sacral Plexus), 3. Nabhi Chakra (Solar Plexus), 4. Hridaya Chakra (Heart Plexus), 5. Kantha Chakra (Vishuddhi Chakra), 6. Ajna Chakra (Brow Plexus), 7. Sahasrāra Chakra (Crown Chakra).

These chakras are also called lotuses and power centres. During the state of samādhi, lotus flower is seen by practitioners at the location of these chakras. Special subtle powers are present in these chakras. The structure of these chakras is different from each other. These chakras are also of different density levels compared to of one another i.e. there is difference of subtlety. There are different deities associated with these chakras. These chakras are related to Sushumna Nadi i.e. the Sushumna Nadi touches these chakras. Sushumna Nadi affects these chakras; in the same way, these chakras cast their effect on the Sushumna Nadi.

i. **Mūlādhāra Chakra** – This chakra is situated at the base of the spine and above the anus. The base of the spine is jaggy or pointed. This chakra lies a little above the pointed part at the widened region. A lotus with four petals is present at this chakra. The god of this chakra is Lord Ganesha.

ii. **Svādhiṣṭhāna Chakra** – This chakra is situated a little above the Mūlādhāra Chakra, behind the reproductive organ. This chakra contains a lotus with six petals. The god of this chakra is Lord Brahma.

iii. **Nabhi Chakra** – This chakra is situated in the spinal column, just behind the navel. It contains a lotus with ten petals. The god of this chakra is Lord Vishnu.

iv. **Hridaya Chakra** – This chakra is situated in the spinal column behind the heart. It has a twelve-petalled lotus. The god of this chakra is Lord Rudra.

v. **Kantha (Throat) Chakra** – This chakra is situated in the throat. It consists of a lotus having sixteen petals. The god of this chakra is Jīvā, implying that it is the place of jīvā.

vi. **Ajna Chakra** – This chakra is located a little above the centre of the eyebrows. There exists lotus with two petals on this chakra. The god of this chakra is Lord Shiva.

vii. **Sahasrāra Chakra** – This chakra is situated on the top of the head i.e. above the Brahmarandhra Dwaar. There exists a thousand-petalled lotus on this chakra. The god of this chakra is Nirguna Brahm.

The density of the chakras above the Mūlādhāra gradually goes on decreasing successively. Due to the decrease in the density of chakras, their pervasiveness increases successively. So the density of the Mūlādhāra Chakra is higher than the other chakras. The density of the Sahasrāra Chakra, situated at the top, is the lowest. This chakra evolves in the last birth of a person. This chakra is the ultimate volume of knowledge.

These chakras are situated in the subtle body. The subtle body remains situated in the gross body. That is why the feeling of unfoldment of these chakras is felt in the physical body. It appears that these chakras are situated in the gross body while these are situated in the subtle body. These chakras are also envisioned by the sādhakas in the form of lotuses. Subtle energies remain present on each petal of these lotuses. When, by practice, these chakras evolves, then the subtle energies become functional. If you wish to unfold these chakras by trāṭaka, make efforts to do so only when your ability is above than the chakra you wish to open, otherwise it will not be possible. If your ability exceeds to that chakra, even then too, there will also be a problem that the method to unfold these chakras should be known. The way to open up a chakra has to be learnt from the guru. Be aware of one more thing regarding these chakras, these chakras remain in dormant state in a normal human being and are also covered with Tamo-guna. To activate these chakras, their sequential evolution is necessary. Just like so long as the bud of rose will not be developed, it can't blossom as a flower. The development of a bud goes on continuously and as the right time comes it can be able to blossom as a flower after its full development. If the bud is not developed, it can't evolve to a flower. In the same way, it should be understood about these chakras. The chakras are also evolved with the help of practicing yoga and devotion also. So long as the chakra is not developed with practice, how can it be opened?

If chakras have to be opened through trāṭaka, then such person will have to resort to meditation etc. for this purpose. The practitioner of trāṭaka, who has not practiced yoga, he is not even supposed to think of opening chakras or the person who has special mastery over trāṭaka can only open these chakras. In this way, only four chakras can be opened. These are— Mūlādhāra Chakra, Svādhiṣṭhāna Chakra, Nabhi Chakra and Hridaya Chakra. The chakras above these four can't be opened. Some seekers, whose chakras are not even opened, yet they think that their chakras are opened.

The practitioner of yoga, whose Kantha (Throat) Chakra is opened, if his Kundalini is ugra and has good practice of trāṭaka, he can open four chakras of a seeker by shaktipāta slowly after some time or in few days. In this process, a lot of the yoga-bala will be spent and Tamo-guna on himself situated on the opened chakras have to be borne by him. While performing these types of tasks, the guru himself has to bear the Karma and impurity of the seeker.

You might have understood the meaning of these lines that at what stage trāṭaka should be used. The human being who has followed a little bit of practice of trāṭaka, he himself will get its benefit, but he can't benefit others with that practice. The practitioner who has not evolved spiritually, but has only attained perfection in trāṭaka and has practiced to perform only material tasks, those persons will be successful in performing material tasks or in showing miracles. If born as a human being, the objective should not be merely to achieve material eminence only, because material superiority will be helpful only till he is alive. The journey afterwards is too long and the load of your karma will also be loaded on you. One who has evolved spiritually along with the practice of trāṭaka, such a practitioner can do welfare of the society. He has the ability to perform spiritual tasks. By doing these Karmas, one gets the Urdhva Lokas (higher subtle worlds) even after death. Such a person has the capability to do philanthropy in worldly and spiritual fields. Such person should not manifest worldly miracles. He should use his power of trāṭak for the welfare of human beings.

The sādhakas who have opened their Brahmarandhra by practicing yoga and whose Kundalini has become stable by completing its full journey, they can perform various tasks by trāṭak. Even arduous tasks can also be performed with the help of trāṭaka according to their ability. These acts are not known to others, as the sādhaka just sees through his eyes and makes samkalpa to do the work in his mind. Jīvanmukta yogi can perform most of his tasks through trāṭaka, because the purity of his chitta is at a very high level.

18.9 Attaining Siddhi (Mystical Powers) by Trataka

Many of the seekers follow their practice of trāṭaka only by keeping in mind that siddhi can be attained by trāṭaka and start its practice. After sometime, they begin to think as to why siddhi is not achieved by the practice of trāṭaka.

There are two bodies that exist in the gross body of human beings. These are the subtle body and the causal body. The subtle body is pervaded within the gross body and is related to the subtle world, because the formation of these two (subtle world & subtle body) is from the five

tattvas. That is why the density of both of these is identical to one another. As the practitioner evolves his inner self by being introverted through practice, his realization of the subtle world begins accordingly. The chakras are also evolved according to the subtle development. When, by the evolution of chakras, this development is almost accomplished, the chakra is unfolded and the energies situated on that chakra begin to be activated. First of all, the Mūlādhāra Chakra is opened, because the density of this chakra is higher than the other chakras situated in the subtle body. In other words, as soon as the subtle body begins to be evolved with practice, then the Mūlādhāra Chakra also starts to be affected. As long as the subtle body does not start to evolve, the chakras remain dormant, there is no effect on them. As long as the practice of seeker is within the realm of his gross body, till then his practice remains confined to the material world related to the material things. There is no meaning of subtle development till that time.

What are the symptoms when a practitioner becomes introverted towards the subtle body. During practice, when the external senses automatically starts becoming introverted, then slowly and gradually become introverted; the flickering tendency of mind bridles and remain calm for some time. When the seeker, during his practice of trāṭaka, forgets about his body and about all the material things with his gaze fixed on the object on which he is practicing trāṭaka, it marks the sign of his advancement. Follow this type of practice for a long time. One has always to maintain patience while doing such practice and has to continue it with complete determination. Eradicate the feeling of enmity and selfishness from the mind, because the chitta is affected by doing so. The seekers also follow different types of sadhanas along with the practice of trāṭaka concurrently. The seekers of satvik path do not perform sadhana just to attain siddhis, because their goal is to be established in the Chetan Tattva or to be one with the Godhead.

18.10 Use of Trataka on the Crowd

When the practitioners of trāṭaka become mature by practicing on trees, stars and the sun etc.,

the capability to produce far-reaching effects by trāṭaka starts coming in them. To influence people at far-off distance, practice of trataka has to be done on the distant objects. Along with this type of practice, trāṭaka should also be used upon a person who is away, because success in such kind of practice is achieved with time.

Enter your will-power by means of majestic blue rays emitted from the eyes into the back portion of the head of the person moving away, and then send your message to his brain. Initially, your message will not have any effect; keep sending this message again and again. After doing so for a few days, it will start to have effect on that person. Similarly, try this on the person coming far in front towards you, your experiment will begin to succeed gradually on doing so. You will see that the person is doing the same as you sent the message. This type of experiment may not have the same effect on all persons, i.e. some persons will be affected by your experiment, and on some others it will not have any effect. The reason for this is that purity and impurity of the chitta of all individuals is different according to their karmas. Such types of experiments have to be done for several months; only then success can be possible. The seeker should not be disheartened on failure of his experiments, rather he should continue.

In such experiments, success and failure depends on one's own ability — how much the experimenter is spiritually advanced, what is the level of purity of his chitta, what is his behaviour in the world, how does he live his material life, whether he observes celibacy etc. If the above things are favorable, his samkalpa will be extremely powerful. The procedure above is more helpful for hypnotism, but the great yogis will not need to do so that they apply their experiments in such a way. The path of yogis is spiritual. God-oriented yogi always remains involved in human welfare. The yogi who has achieved greatness, attracts the crowd only on seeing it or on having a look all around the crowd while preaching, even if he has not practiced trāṭaka much. The secret behind his success is the practice of yoga done by him. There is only a thought of human welfare in his chitta.

In the year 1893, Swami Vivekananda went to America; while preaching he applied shaktipāta by trāṭaka on the entire crowd present there. The crowd influenced by trāṭaka, kept listening his discourse being spell bound. Some people were influenced so much with his speech that they became his followers. It is written in the Bible- —Wherever Jesus Christ used to go, the crowd used to follow him. There have been some saints, who have not practiced trāṭaka, but the worldly people became very influenced by the rays emitted out from their eyes, they used to lose their presence of mind and would become their followers.

18.11 Changing Negative Thoughts by Trataka

Trāṭaka is such a science, by which various types of tasks can be performed. It is quite important to know as to how trāṭaka is to be used, so that success can be achieved in any activity. First of all, it is significant to have yoga-bala, because all the activities are performed by it. The practice of trāṭaka must be enormous. In order to perform any work, it is necessary to know the method to do it. If any of these has lacked or is lacking, failure may be met in accomplishment of any task.

Sometimes there are some tasks for which there is not much importance of having yoga-bala, e.g. hypnotism etc. Yoga-bala is inevitable if the seeker wants to remove negative thought of anybody. If yoga-bala is used, then success will surely be achieved and he will also remain normal. If only hypnotism is used to eliminate the negative thought, then so long as hypnotism will have its effect, all will be well, but as soon as the effect of hypnotism is lost, the person can regain his previous negative thoughts. But if yoga-bala is used to change his thinking, it will begin to be purified due to that yoga-bala and impurity will begin to decline. It is not so with a hypnotized person, because impurity (Tamo-guna) remains in his thoughts. But with trataka, the negative thoughts of the practitioners are permanently changed to positive thoughts.

Bibliography

Amai, Dr. Krithi. " A Comparative Clinical Study to evaluate the efficacy of Jyothi Trataka and Eye exercises in the management of Prathama Patalagata Timira w.s.r. to simple Myopia", Dissertation Submitted to the Rajiv Gandhi University of Health Sciences, Bengaluru, 2017–2018.

Bhadra, Champak and Dr. Kallol Chatterjee "Effect of Trataka on pulse rate of college level male students", International Journal of Yogic, Human Movement and Sports Sciences 2018; 3(1): 873–875

Bhavanani, Yogacharya Ananda Balayogi. "Meditation: The Inner Yoga", January 2011, https://www.researchgate.net/publication/237079027

Chang, Kang-Ming, Miao-Tien Wu Chueh. "Using Eye Tracking to Assess Gaze Concentration in Meditation", Sensors 2019, 19, 1612; doi:10.3390/s19071612 www.mdpi.com/journal/sensors

Choudhary, Dr. Rajeev et. al. "Effect of Prandharana and Tratak on Orientation Ability of Physical Education Students", April 2017. https://www.researchgate.net/publication/317936749

Dayanidy, Yogachemmal Sri G and Yogacharya Dr. Ananda Balayogi Bhavanani, "Yoga Practical Notes: For students of CFY, CFYT, CCAY, CCAYT, PGDYT & MPhil (YT)"

Dienstmann, Giovanni. "Trataka Meditation: Still Eyes, Still Mind", http://liveanddare.com/trataka/. "Bringing Meditation and Personal Growth to one million people" (Live and Dare mission).

Dudeja, Jai Paul. "The Third Eye: A Spiritual Laser for Stimulating Inner Awakening", GenNext Publication, New Delhi, 2019.

Dudeja, Jai Paul. "Chakras Healing and Kundalini Awakening by Yogic Techniques", Chaukhamba Sanskrit Pratishthan, Delhi, 2021.

Dudeja, Jai Paul. "Meditation Practices across the Globe and their Beneficial Effects", White Falcon Publishing Solutions, Chandigarh, 2021.

Dudeja, Jai Paul. "Scientific Analysis of Mantra-Based Meditation and Its Beneficial Effects: An Overview", International Journal of Advanced Scientific Technologies in Engineering and Management Sciences (IJASTEMS-ISSN: 2454–356X), Vol. 3, Issue 6, June 2017, pp. 21–26.

Dudeja, Jai Paul. "An Overview of Primordial, Apaurusheya, Perennial, Universal 'OM' Mantra and Its Scientific Analysis", International Journal of Current Trends in Science and Technology, (ISSN: 0976–9730), Vol. 7, Issue. 9, Sep 2017, pp 20370–20390.

Gopinathan, G. Kartar Singh Dhiman, and R. Manjusha. "A clinical study to evaluate the efficacy of Trataka Yoga Kriya and eye exercises (non-pharmocological methods) in the management of Timira (Ammetropia and Presbyopia)", Ayu. 2012, Oct-Dec: 33(4), 543–548.

Goswami, Jogiswar and Rakesh Datta, Journal of Advances and Scholarly Researches in Allied Education [JASRAE] (Vol:16/ Issue: 6) DOI: 10.29070/JASRAE

Karmarkar, Kripesh and Dr. Gaurav Pant. "Effect of trataka kriya session on the visual perception of elderly people", International Journal of Yoga, Physiotherapy and Physical Education Online, Volume 2; Issue 2; March 2017; Page No. 45–48.

Schatz, H. and F. Mrndelblatt. "Solar retinopathy from sungazing under the influence of LSD", Brit. J. Ophthal. (1973) 57, 270

Manek, Hira Ratan. Compiled by Vina Parmar. "Living on Sunlight: The Art and Science of Sun Gazing as taught by Hira Ratan Manek, HRM" Living on Sunlight Publishing, Dec 2004.

Muktibodhananda, Swami. "Hatha Yoga Pradipika: Light on Hatha Yoga", Yoga Publications Trust, Munger, Bihar, India, Bihar School of Yoga, 1998.

Nagar, Murari and Sarla Nagar. "Om: One God Universal, A Garland of Holy Offerings: Viveka Leads To Ānanda", Vivekananda Kendra Patrika, Om Shanti Mandiram, Columbia MO, 2001

Niranjan, Swami. "Trataka: Yogic practice of concentration", Sanskriti, 2014.

Pindipol, Dr. Shrinivas S. "Efficacy of Trataka in Tandra Vyadhi", Dissertation for MD, Rajiv Gandhi University of Health Sciences, Bangalore. 2018.

Raghavendra, B.R. and Prashanth Singh. "Immediate effect of yogic visual concentration on cognitive performance", Journal of Traditional and Complementary Medicine 6 (2016) 34–36.

Raghavendra, B.R. and V Ramamurthy "Changes in Heart Rate Variability Following Yogic Visual Concentration (Trataka)", http://www.heartindia.net on Thursday, February 17, 2022, IP: 49.207.214.150.

Rajpoot, Pushp Lata and Pushpa Vaishnav. "Effect of Trataka on Anxiety among Adolescents", World Academy of Science, Engineering and Technology International Journal of Psychological and Behavioral Sciences Vol:8, No:12, 2014

Rathee, Nirmaljit K. and Sudesh Bhardwaj. "Contemporary Yoga Education: Transforming the Body, Mind and Soul", European Scientific Institute, ESI www.euinstitute.net publishing, 2017.

Satyananda, Swami Saraswati. YOGA, Vol. 1, No. 3, 1963.

Sivananda, Sri Swami. "Kundalini Yoga", A Divine Life Society Publication, 1999.

Sivananda, Sri Swami. "Yoga in Daily Life", A Divine Life Society Publication, 1999. Sri Balaji Vidyapeeth, Pondicherry.

Sivananda, Swami. "Concentration & Meditation", The Divine Life Society.

Srinivasulu, Colonel T. "Secrets of Shaktipat and Kundalini Yoga (Volume 3)", 2020 www.sahajananda-ashram.com

Swathi, P. S. Raghavendra Bhat and Apar Avinash Saoji. "Effect of Trataka (Yogic Visual Concentration) on the Performance in the Corsi-Block Tapping Task: A Repeated Measures Study". Front. Psychol. 12:773049. doi: 10.3389/fpsyg.2021.773049

Talwadkar, Shubhada, Aarti Jagannathan, and Nagarathna Raghuram. "Effect of trataka on cognitive functions in the elderly", International Journal of Yoga, Vol. 7, Jul-Dec-2014, 96–102.

Tyagi, Dr. Neelam. "Management of Stress & Frustration-Causes & Remedies" International Journal of Education and Science Research Review E- ISSN 2348–6457, Volume-1, Issue-3 June- 2014 P- ISSN 2349–1817.

Vidyape, Bharati and Gaurav Pant. "Effect of trataka kriya session on the visual perception of elderly people", April 2017. https://www.researchgate.net/publication/316284399

Vivekananda, Swami. "Patanjali Yoga Sutras: Sanskrit text with Translation and Commentary"

Yadav, Saroj. "Yoga: A Healthy Way of Living", A document of The National Council of Educational Research and Training (NCERT)

Yogendra, Shri. "Guide to Yoga Meditation", Yogendra Publication Fund, The Yoga Institute, Bombay. 6th edition, 2000.

Yogi, Anand Ji. "Trataka". Book in Hindi, ISBN 978-93-5291-271-1. Self-Published, Bhargava Press, Prayagraj, Uttar Pradesh.

www.ingramcontent.com/pod-product-compliance
Ingram Content Group UK Ltd.
Pitfield, Milton Keynes, MK11 3LW, UK
UKHW041318060425
5344UKWH00020B/56